LOUIS NOWRA

THE TEMPLE

*un*tapped

ABOUT *UNTAPPED*

Most Australian books ever written have fallen out of print and become unavailable for purchase or loan from libraries. This includes important local and national histories, biographies and memoirs, beloved children's titles, and even winners of glittering literary prizes such as the Miles Franklin Literary Award.

Supported by funding from state and territory libraries, philanthropists and the Australian Research Council, *Untapped* is identifying Australia's culturally important lost books, digitising them, and promoting them to new generations of readers. As well as providing access to lost books and a new source of revenue for their writers, the *Untapped* collaboration is supporting new research into the economic value of authors' reversion rights and book promotion by libraries, and the relationship between library lending and digital book sales. The results will feed into public policy discussions about how we can better support Australian authors, readers and culture.

See untapped.org.au for more information, including a full list of project partners and rediscovered books.

Readers are reminded that these books are products of their time. Some may contain language or reflect views that might now be found offensive or inappropriate.

CONTENTS

The Temple was first performed by the Playbox Theatre Centre on 27 July 1993 at the CUB Malthouse with the following cast:

LAURIE BLAKE
Mark Little

BRENDA BLAKE, LORNA ST JOHN
Genevieve Picot

NICK ALBERT
Anthony Wong

ED, TERRY MACARTHUR, SIMON MACKENZIE, DAVID ASLOP, REGGIE
Joseph Spano

JANE, MIRANDA WILSON, HELEN BLAKE, ARAB POOL CLEANER
Nikki Coghill

SIR THOMAS MACARTHUR, HENRY, FREDDIE ARROW
Tony Hawkins

SIR JAMES WILSON, BARRY ST JOHN, RESTAURANT PATRON, BERNARD
Neill Gladwin

Directed by Bruce Myles

Designed by Judith Cobb

Lighting by Glenn Hughes

CHARACTERS

LAURIE BLAKE
BRENDA BLAKE, his wife
HELEN BLAKE, their daughter
NICK ALBERT, Laurie's assistant
JANE, model maker
SIR THOMAS BURCHETT
TERRY BURCHETT, his son
SIR JAMES, member of the Burchett Board
ED, slaughterman
MIRANDA, art expert
SIMON MACKENZIE, banker
SAINT JOHN, New Zealand businessman
LORNA SAINT JOHN, his wife
HENRY, head Waiter at Pandoras
DAVID ASLOP, editor of *The Observer*
FREDDIE ARROW, British businessman
REGGIE, English head 'Beater'
WEDDING WAITER
WOMAN
ARABIC POOL CLEANER

SETTING

Australia, France, England, Libya. Time, 1980s

ACT ONE

SCENE ONE · THE SCENT OF BLOOD

The abattoirs. Day. Men dressed in blood splattered white boiler suits come and go carrying pig and sheep carcasses, newly killed, over their shoulders. In the distance the sound of frightened pigs. A man, NICK ALBERT, *enters, dressed in a suit. In his early twenties he is new to something like this and is at a bit of a loss.* ED, *wearing a blood splattered white pair of overalls and gumboots, passes by.*

NICK

Excuse me.

ED

Yeh?

NICK

I'm after Mr Blake. The staff upstairs said he'd be down here.

ED

Yeh, he likes the killing floors. In there.

NICK

Thank you.

[*He starts to go*]

ED

Where you going?

NICK

To talk to him.

ED

You can't go in there dressed like that. You'll be covered

in blood by the time you open the door.

NICK

I wonder if you could tell him I'm here. My name's Nick Albert from Esko merchant bank.

ED

Sure.

NICK

[*as* ED *starts to go*] Excuse me ...

ED

Yeh.

NICK

Is Mr Blake actually in there killing the pigs himself?

ED

Helping out. He says he doesn't want to lose his touch.

[NICK *nods as if it makes sense and* ED *goes. A young woman,* JANE HUDSON, *dressed plainly and wearing overalls, enters.*]

JANE

Could you give me a hand?

NICK

Me?

JANE

Just for a moment.

[*He exits with her as* BRENDA BLAKE, *wearing leopard skin pants and a silk green top—a walking fashion disaster—enters*]

BRENDA

[*to herself*] Where the bloody hell is he? Laurie! [*No answer*] Laurie!

[ED *enters*]

Ed, where's the hubby?

ED

In there cutting a few throats. Did you see a young guy from a merchant bank?

BRENDA

Couldn't give a stuff. I'm looking for the keys to the Rolls. Maybe he's left them in his office. [*She heads off as* NICK *and* JANE *enter, he helping her to bring on a table which has the model of a tourist resort on it*]

ED

Hey, mate.

NICK

Yes?

ED

Laurie will be out in a mo.

NICK

Thanks.

[*The couple put down the table*]

JANE

God knows why he wants it down here instead of inside his office. It stinks to high heaven.

NICK

Yeh, I don't know how you could work in that smell.

What is it?

JANE

I made it. It's a model of a tourist resort in Northern Queensland.

NICK

It looks like a Japanese village.

JANE

That's the idea, Blakey thinks that Japanese tourists like the familiar when they holiday. I forgot the Shinto shrine.

[She *leaves.* ED *is curious and wanders over.*]

ED

Laurie's village for the slant eyes? [*Pretends to jerk off, eyes half closed*] Hey, I'm turning Japanese. [NICK *is queasy at the racial term*] He told me about it at the pub the other night.

[LAURIE *enters, in blood splattered overalls, grinning from ear to ear*]

LAURIE

God, I love the smell of the abattoir. It smells of ... money.

ED

This is the merchant bank guy.

LAURIE

G'day.

[*He shakes* NICK's *hand, as* ED *leaves*]

Laurie Blake.

NICK

Nick Albert.

[LAURIE's *attention is taken by the model.* NICK *realises he has a bloody hand now and wipes it with his white linen handkerchief*]

LAURIE

Ah, the Japs will wet their kimonos over this.

NICK

You deal with them?

LAURIE

Sell them tendons for their tennis rackets.

NICK

Tendons?

LAURIE

They don't like artificial strings, they like to know they're playing with real meat. Reminds them of the war, I suppose. Where's Jane?

NICK

She had to get a temple from her car.

LAURIE

I discovered her doing Myer's Christmas windows. I sensed she had a bit of showmanship. The Japs like that. Because they're small they can identify with models. Hey, where's your boss?

NICK

Mr Esko couldn't come.

LAURIE

So, who are you?

NICK

His assistant.

LAURIE

What kind of fuckin' stunt is that?

NICK

Excuse me?

BRENDA

[*entering*] Laurie!

LAURIE

[*to* NICK] Jeez, she can cut steel with that voice.

BRENDA

The keys for the Roller.

LAURIE

I gave them to my secretary.

BRENDA

As a trade off for a poke.

LAURIE

Christ, Brenda. This is ... [He *has forgotten the name*]

NICK

Nick Albert.

BRENDA

[*lying*] Pleased to meet you. [*She sees his blood splattered handkerchief*] Got your rags on today?

[LAURIE *rolls his eyes*]

LAURIE

Had a few champers with the girls, did you?

BRENDA

Yeh and I'm late. I have to pick up Helen from the airport.

LAURIE

Why not take a taxi?

BRENDA

I want to pick her up in the Rolls. She'd like that.

[BRENDA *heads off*]

LAURIE

My daughter's back from a school excursion. I thought sending her to a private school would be good. But all she does is go on excursions and develop a toffee-table accent. So I didn't get the fuckin' money?

NICK

Excuse me?

LAURIE

[*taking off his overalls, revealing a suit underneath*] Sending an assistant can only mean one thing—Esko's not going to give me the money.

[*Pause*]

Right?

NICK

He felt it was too great a risk.

LAURIE

He's the type of bloke who runs around all day holding

his cock for fear of risking losing it. You've got to lay your balls on the line in this world Nick. How old are you?

NICK

Twenty-four.

LAURIE

How old's Esko?

NICK

In his sixties.

LAURIE

And so's the rest of the top boys in the bank, right? [NICK *nods*] The old, old boys network. That's what's wrong with this country. It's stagnant. Old. Youth like you can't do what we want to and then we're too old to put our visions into practice once we get in power. You'll be pushing up daisies before they allow you into the boardroom. You don't have a chance. [*A beat*] University educated?

NICK

Yes.

LAURIE

You don't need a degree to cut a pig's throat. So why won't fucking Esko give me the money I want.

NICK

You're asking for tens of millions.

LAURIE

So?

NICK

This abattoir is not worth tens of millions.

LAURIE

But if I buy the brewery, the merchant bank gets its money back.

NICK

How?

LAURIE

I'll flog most of the assets. Sell the hop farms, the pubs but keep the brewery.

NICK

Mr Esko thinks you'll be too much in debt and that if you can't sell those assets the bank will be owed millions.

LAURIE

I'll sell 'em—I can sell mountaineering holidays to quadriplegics. What Esko doesn't realise is that old fogies like him will be killed in the stampede to build this country anew. Smell it, Nick. Smell the air. What do you smell?

NICK

Blood.

LAURIE

And you know what the scent of new blood means, Nick? A new era! This is a revolution!

[ED *passes*]

Get Shirl to send me down some sandwiches, Ed.

ED

What sort, Laurie?

LAURIE

Pig with a bit of blood. [*To* NICK] You know what Ed and I get off on. I built this new abattoir a few hundred meters from the local Mosque. When the wind comes from the south, it blows the smell of pig right into the Mosque. Drives the Moslems mad. [*He laughs, but* NICK *finds it hard to*] You want to be successful?

NICK

Doesn't everybody?

LAURIE

Well, you won't at Esko's. The thing is, Nick. I've put a bit of money where my mouth is, unlike a lot of other people, and I've bought a fair few shares of Burchett's brewery, believing that Esko was forward looking like me. So I stand to take a bit of a caning. It's no sob story, it's just the facts. You don't think he'll change his mind.

NICK

You're not his style, he said.

LAURIE

Yeh, I'm brash, forward looking. [*More to himself, angrily*] Fuck! [*Looking at model*] I'm going to be fucking out a fortune—where in the hell will I get the money for this?

NICK

You've started building it?

LAURIE

I just have to give the whistle to start it. A watertight contract: the Japs buy the land, I build the resort. They've fulfilled their part of the bargain. Fuck! What a day! The wife takes the Rolls—I mean the only time my secretary will hump me is if we do it in the Roller. [NICK's *mind is somewhere else*] I only leased it to get into her pants. Not that she wears any.

NICK

Go to a bank.

LAURIE

What?

NICK

The banks are going to be deregulated. If you got in first, they'll loan you the money. It's going to be a revolution in banking. They'll think of the huge profits that can be made on bridging loans for takeovers.

LAURIE

You think so?

NICK

Others can't see it, but I can. The clever ones well know that foreign banks will come in and want to loan money—Australians will have to compete. For the first time there will be competition. The way the Americans do it.

LAURIE

Esko given you a car?

NICK

I use a company car.

LAURIE

I'll give you a Porsche all your own.

NICK

That information's free.

LAURIE

You join me and I'll triple what you're earning.

NICK

I really don't think so—

LAURIE

What's your problem?

NICK

The risks—you're really out on a limb and there's a question of integrity.

LAURIE

Of what?

NICK

I did some research—Mr Esko wanted it.

LAURIE

What sort of research?

NICK

Into past financial dealings, that sort of thing.

LAURIE

And?

NICK

You were once fined—

LAURIE

Bloody railroaded, Nick. Jesus, I was a teenager. But I had a vision—I knew I wanted to be rich—

NICK

They were pensioners.

LAURIE

I was screwed! It was me who was screwed. Bought five

hundred Hungarian TV sets, how was I to know the Communists only have one channel. And what's the diff, anyway? All channels spew out the same junk—at least they didn't have to get up and change the channel and have some heart attack. Did they? Probably saved a few senior citizens their lives.

NICK

You know, it doesn't go down well with someone like Mr Esko.

LAURIE

Well, bully for him. He belongs in another world. The future needs people like us with initiative. Whata you say to that?

[*Pause*]

They'll never let you in their boardroom, Nick. I'll give you all the power you want. At your age in America you'd be on the top floor in the Gods, an important wheeler and dealer. Here? Because companies are run by dead wood; a messenger boy. Like Jesus, we'll smash the temple.

NICK

I don't know, Mr Blake—

LAURIE

Laurie, old mate. Laurie. We'll conquer them all, it'll be like Gallipoli.

NICK

We lost Gallipoli.

LAURIE

Yeh, well, this time we'll win Gallipoli.

NICK

Burchett brewery is huge.

LAURIE

Then we'll be like a mouse swallowing a cat. [A *beat*] Look, join me and I'll throw in a Hungarian TV.

[NICK *looks at* LAURIE *to see whether he is serious. He is not.* LAURIE *laughs and so does* NICK *despite himself,* JANE *enters with the Shinto temple*]

JANE

Sorry, Mr Blake, I had to go and get this.

[LAURIE *holds out his hand for it, she hands it over.*]

A Shinto temple.

LAURIE

Nick and I smash temples.

[*He throws it on the ground. Much to* JANE's *horror it smashes into pieces.*]

SCENE TWO · BIRDS OF A FEATHER

A giant walk-in aviary. SIR THOMAS BURCHETT *is among his birds, putting seed into their trays. He wears a hat, which is bird shit splattered. He is delighted to be with them, humming along with the general, soft murmuring sounds, broken by the occasional hard call of a parrot.*

THOMAS

[*talking to birds*] Who's the beautiful bird? Who makes the gods close their eyes at such beauty?

[SIR JAMES *enters*]

JAMES

Hello, Tom.

THOMAS

[*surprised to see him*] Wasn't expecting you, James. Put on that stuff over there or you'll be covered in poop in next to no time. Over there.

[SIR JAMES *goes over to the wall where there hangs a coat and hat, both bird shit splattered*]

JAMES

[*dressing*] Couldn't find you inside. Your butler said you'd be out here.

THOMAS

I spend a lot of time in my aviary now.

[SIR JAMES *is uninterested in the birds and finds himself having to duck one*]

The birds of paradise are my favourite. Once Thelma passed away the hobby has become an obsession. Why doesn't *The Herald* write more about birds?

JAMES

There doesn't seem a call for it, Tom.

THOMAS

Nonsense, I own a large part of *The Herald*, I can do what I like. Tell Aslop to get a bird correspondent. [*A beat*] Did you see Terry on your way in?

JAMES

No.

THOMAS

He's running late. I know why. He hates seeing me. [*Amused*] A son his age scared of his father. You think he's one of those ...

JAMES

Hard to tell nowadays, Tom.

THOMAS

Maybe impotent. Which would be worse. To have an impotent son or a nancy one.

JAMES

[*trying to get things back on track*] I was wanting to talk to you about a problem, rather personal, Tom—

THOMAS

The Armenians apparently strangled both sorts of sons. The father did it, which is only right. Anything earth shattering at last night's board meeting?

JAMES

Well, there was some interesting news. Someone has bought nine per cent of Burchett's brewery.

THOMAS

[*unconcerned*] Take over my company? Who? Who has the money?

JAMES

It seems the person doing it doesn't have the money.

THOMAS

What sort of nonsense is that?

JAMES

I ran into Esko at the Club last night ... apparently this idiot has bought nine per cent of the brewery as a prelude to a takeover but hasn't got the money for the other forty-two per cent, so he asked Esko for a bridging loan who, of course, laughed him out of his office.

THOMAS

Esko buy that stud up north? [JAMES *nods*] Still playing the gee-gees yourself, Jimmy?

JAMES

It's a hobby.

THOMAS

The way you play it, it's a disease.

[TERRY *enters shyly and almost wanting to be unnoticed, automatically puts on a coat and hat to protect himself.* THOMAS *glances at his son,* TERRY *tries to avoid eye contact*]

JAMES

Hello, Terry.

TERRY

Sir James.

[THOMAS *pretends not to have noticed the arrival of his son and goes back to the subject of the takeover*]

THOMAS

Who is this idiot?

JAMES

[*thinking he means* TERRY] Idiot?

THOMAS

[*irritated*] The fool with the takeover bid.

JAMES

A fellow called Laurie Blake.

THOMAS

Never heard of him.

JAMES

Owns an abattoir.

THOMAS

An abattoir? So what's going to happen?

JAMES

Esko's guess is that Blake will be forced to sell the shares at a much lower price than he paid for them and will probably be ruined.

[*A beat*]

THOMAS

Why would someone with no money attempt to buy the brewery? He must be mad.

JAMES

Apparently. Part criminal too.

THOMAS

[*horrified*] A convict buying the brewery. It's been in our family for four generations and it was started by a free settler, not a convict or emancipist.

JAMES

He's not a convicted criminal. I thought the name rang a bell. I asked around the traps. He was warned off Australian racecourses for three years after stewards discovered that the transmission of a race from Bathurst was delayed while punters made their bets. He was said to be among the huge winners. They couldn't prove anything ...

THOMAS

But it was him?

JAMES

That's the word.

THOMAS

Horse racing seems to attract a singularly unattractive group of people.

JAMES

Some of the best people in society—people like Esko. [JAMES *guides* THOMAS *out of* TERRY's *hearing*] I know your attitude, Thomas—

THOMAS

You've wasted all your money on horses. At least you could have done it on birds—

JAMES

Not much money in bird racing, Thomas.

THOMAS

I know why you're here, Jimmy, from the moment you entered. Nothing to do with the board meeting.

JAMES

A little, just to tide me over.

THOMAS

No, for your own good, no. I promised your sister. She's scared of dying destitute.

JAMES

You don't know how serious it is this time.

THOMAS

You've squandered your inheritance, Jimmy. No. [A *beat*] No. If you try to sting me any more I will cut you off the board. You must learn temperance.

JAMES

[*nodding, biting his tongue*] You're right, Thomas.

THOMAS

Stay away from those nags.

JAMES

Absolutely, Thomas. Best I go. [*To* TERRY] Bye, Terry.

[JAMES *goes. Silence as the father goes around feeding his birds,* TERRY *waits nervously in the awkward silence*]

THOMAS

You're late.

TERRY

I got the times mixed up.

[THOMAS *shakes his head, exasperated with his son*]

THOMAS

You were bloody late for your own mother's funeral too.

[*Silence*]

What I should have done was stop your grandfather's inheritance. You'll lose it like James lost his family's fortune.

TERRY

I don't gamble.

THOMAS

You don't work either. You could be working at the brewery.

TERRY

You'd just yell at me as you've always done.

THOMAS

You little—[*He is going to yell at him but it is too important*]

[*Pause*]

[*Calmer*] Your mother's death made me aware of just how mortal I am. The heart has a will of its own. And I'll have to make my will.

TERRY

You've cut me in and out every year.

THOMAS

You're still in. [TERRY *shrugs*] Don't you understand what I'm saying. You're my only flesh and blood. The name Burchett means a lot in Australia. It's a business name made flesh and blood.

TERRY

What makes you think I would want to.

THOMAS

Because you're blood.

TERRY

From when?

THOMAS

What's got into you, why are you so negative?

TERRY

You're feeling mortal and now you start to be kind. You've never shown me any interest or love.

THOMAS

Great families are not about love, they're about the past connecting to the future. What about *The Herald.* [TERRY *looks at him quizzically*] We have part of that. I can get you working there. You'd like newspapers.

TERRY

No.

THOMAS

[*angrily*] For Christ's sake! All you bloody do is travel and collect art. Now I hear you're into abo art! What about our family! [*He calms down because he knows he has to*] Don't make a decision now.

[*Pause*]

Great families are about ties to the family.

TERRY

[*staring at the birds*] I don't care about family. You didn't start calling me a part of the family until you needed me.

THOMAS

Look at me, for once in your life, look at me. Look me straight in the eye like a real man, tell me what you really feel.

TERRY

[*looking him straight in the eye*] I see a scared, old man. Blood is thicker than water, you've always told me that, but you can at least drink water. [*He goes*]

SCENE THREE · STALLIONS AND MARES

The racecourse. Day. Concourse. Distant sound of P.A. system announcing the sixth race in ten minutes. NICK *looks at his form guide but can't concentrate.*

NICK

[*To himself*] Why did I agree to meet him here?—I hate horse racing. Smell of horseshit and women wearing too much perfume. Just say to him: 'I don't want your Porsche.' It's probably leased anyway.

[BRENDA *enters, again a fashion disaster but with sunglasses on. She spots* NICK]

BRENDA

Hi, ya, spunk.

NICK

Mrs Blake.

BRENDA

Brenda. Brenda. You seen my better half?

NICK

He's having a word to a jockey.

BRENDA

Christ, he was warned off the course for three years and the moment he's back—people will think suspicious thoughts, Nick. Still, Laurie has never worried about that. Never lost a night's sleep over anything. One time we were an inch to bankruptcy—it had to be decided the next day. He slept like a baby. I couldn't sleep a wink. Had bags under my eyes like saddlebags. You know what jockey he was talking to?

NICK

No.

BRENDA

You look worried. Laurie's got your balls on the line, eh?

NICK

I've told him I want to remain at Esko's.

BRENDA

Why? Laurie'll make you rich. How's the Porsche? Mongrels to corner.

NICK

I don't drive it.

BRENDA

Nancy, are you?

NICK

What I mean is that it would obligate me to work for Laurie if I did.

BRENDA

I'll tell you something, Nick. Laurie's got more get up and go in his little finger than people have in their whole body. You know the abattoir. He didn't have any money to buy it, but he managed to convince a jew to put up the money. Now I don't mean to be anti-semantic, but if you can convince a jew to give you money when you have no real collateral, then you've got something special. And let me tell you something else, Nick. You're young. You've got brains, but you don't clang as you walk.

[LAURIE *enters with a large grin*]

LAURIE

We're looking good.

[LAURIE *takes out a roll of money and gives it to* BRENDA]

Put it all on Byzantine Girl. He's a cert.

BRENDA

How many bookmakers.

LAURIE

Do three.

[BRENDA *goes*]

Love it, love it. The colour. The money. Horses toey up at the start. Thunder of the hooves. Sweating on a horse and a dwarf and pow—my horse hitting the finishing line. Love it.

[MIRANDA *enters, looking for her uncle*]

NICK

There's a couple of things I have to tell you, Laurie.

MIRANDA

[*spotting* NICK] Nick!

NICK

[*embarrassed to be seen with* LAURIE] Miranda!

[*They peck one another on the cheek*]

Miranda, this is Laurie Blake.

LAURIE

G'day.

MIRANDA

[*condescendingly*] Hello, Mr ...

LAURIE

Blake.

MIRANDA

[*turning to* NICK, *ignoring* LAURIE] I've lost my uncle. [*Spotting* SIR JAMES] Oh, there he is. [*To herself*] Slickered again. [*Warmly to* NICK] We must have dinner. [*Coldly to* LAURIE] Nice to meet you. [*She goes*]

LAURIE

[*impressed by her*] Who the fuck was that?

NICK

Miranda Wilson—from one of Australia's best families—we went to university together. She's a brilliant art historian.

LAURIE

Like a nun, needs a good clean out of her plumbing. [*A beat, not noticing* NICK's *appalled expression*] Is that Sir James Wilson—that's her uncle? [NICK *nods*] He's on the board of Burchett's brewery. He's got four per cent of shares in it. Married twice. Second wife dead. One sister. Geelong Grammar. Hobbies: Polo, horse racing.

NICK

You've studied up on him?

LAURIE

All of them. *Who's Who* is the only book I've read from cover to cover.

[LAURIE *watches* MIRANDA *engaged in deep conversation with her uncle as they study the form guide*]

What a great rump she's got. You know I once had an idea for women's dresses: have a horse's tail hanging from the bum. I have ideas all the time.

NICK

I had a talk to the State Bank.

LAURIE

Sir James successful with the ponies?

NICK

Esko calls him a mug punter. Loses a lot apparently. [*A beat*] The point is, Laurie. The State Bank said no.

LAURIE

[*concerned*] No?

NICK

They wouldn't give you the loan—for the same reasons.

LAURIE

It's full of fuddy duddies. Let's try the ANZ.

NICK

We'll get the same reaction.

LAURIE

Bring the ANZ guy up to our offices. Can you get a hooker?

NICK

A hooker?

LAURIE

Forget it for the moment. Get the most gung-ho guy you can find. A young guy like yourself who wants to kill for it. Let's see a *Who's Who* entry in the flesh. [*They walk over to* SIR JAMES] Sir James Wilson?

SIR JAMES

Yes?

LAURIE

Laurie Blake.

SIR JAMES

[*drunk and surprised to be shaking hands with him*] Hello.

LAURIE

My partner, Nick Albert.

[NICK *is embarrassed to be seen with* LAURIE]

NICK

No, no, he's joking. I'm just advising him for the moment.

LAURIE

He's holding out for more money.

SIR JAMES

My niece.

LAURIE

We've met. The best filly on the course.

[MIRANDA *is appalled at the clumsiness of the flirtation*]

MIRANDA

What are you—best gelding?

[*Her words are water off a duck's back as far as* LAURIE *is concerned*]

LAURIE

A betting man, Sir James?

SIR JAMES

Bit of a flutter occasionally.

LAURIE

Don't we all.

SIR JAMES

[*Suddenly realising*] You're Laurie Blake!

LAURIE

[*pleased*] Yeh.

SIR JAMES

You were warned off the course.

LAURIE

Three years ago, but my suspension finished this morning. What are you going for on the sixth?

SIR JAMES

Byzantine Girl.

LAURIE

[*laughing*] You're not!

SIR JAMES

[*Worried*] Why?

LAURIE

Couldn't get into a canter if you told him he was going to the soap factory.

SIR JAMES

Look, I really don't want to talk to you. Miranda! [*He*

grabs her hand] Let's seek some fresh air.

LAURIE

I'm placing a nice sum on Unforgiven.

[SIR JAMES *starts to head off with* MIRANDA *pretending not to listen as* LAURIE *calls after her.*]

It's going to be an outstanding galloper. From what I heard it had a sensational track gallop the other morning. Over 1800 metres. Worked eight metres out on the course proper and ran 1:57.5 with a final 600 metres sectional in 33.75.

[SIR JAMES *has slowed down on hearing the information and stops.*]

SIR JAMES

[*Astonished*] 33.75!

LAURIE

The trainer thought his stop watch had gone on the blink.

SIR JAMES

Unforgiven?

LAURIE

Look at the odds.

[NICK *is puzzled as to why* LAURIE *is recommending a horse he has not bet on*]

SIR JAMES

If you're going for it, Mr Blake.

LAURIE

Laurie. In a big way, Sir James. If we win, we're millionaires.

SIR JAMES

I'd better place my bet.

LAURIE

Absolutely.

SIR JAMES

Come on, Miranda, I feel lucky.

MIRANDA

Don't bet it all, Uncle. Promise me.

[SIR JAMES *hurries off*]

NICK

Why aren't you betting on Unforgiven?

LAURIE

It's a dog: I made up the figures. [*To the confused* NICK] We'd better watch the race, old Nick. Place a bet; put everything on Byzantine Girl.

The grandstand. The race is on, on one side of the stage, MIRANDA *and* SIR JAMES *are watching the race.* MIRANDA *is calm, but* SIR JAMES, *although not yelling out, is tense and is urging his horse along,* BRENDA *is screaming out.*

BRENDA

Byzantine Girl! Byzantine Girl!

SIR JAMES

[*softly, but urgently*] Unforgiven ... Unforgiven ...

[NICK *and* LAURIE *arrive*]

LAURIE

Going a beauty!

BRENDA

He's creaming them.

NICK

God, he's fast.

LAURIE

I wouldn't bet on anything else.

BRENDA

You little ripper!

[NICK *gets caught up and starts yelling out with* BRENDA *and* LAURIE. *Byzantine Girl races across the line a clear winner. The trio hug each other. The race caller becomes worried.*]

SIR JAMES

[*Realising he has lost*] Oh, no.

RACECALLER

Byzantine Girl looks in a bit of trouble, folks. That race has taken it out of him. The course record has been at a cost.

BRENDA

Laurie, he looks sick. Really sick.

LAURIE

[*worried himself*] Yeh, yeh.

NICK

What's the problem?

LAURIE

Too big a heart. It really took it out of him.

NICK

Why are they holding up a blanket in front of him?

BRENDA

They've got the vet and the works.

LAURIE

That horse gave its whole heart. So did the jockey. It's a wonder the jockey didn't bloody cark it too. Probably needs a rest.

RACECALLER

There is a protest. Ladies and gentlemen, the protest flag is up. The jockey of Unforgiven has protested against Byzantine Girl's jockey.

SIR JAMES

[*Elated*] Yes ...

MIRANDA

[*not interested, motioning*] Isn't that Lisa Crawford? Her father has a collection as large as Browns.

LAURIE

Quick Brenda, piss off down there and have a word to him.

BRENDA

What?

LAURIE

YOU know how those stewards are. He's in the clear but they like to fuss and they'll put an intolerable strain on his heart. Tell him to take an Asian holiday. As long as he likes; I'll pick up the bill.

[*Used to this,* BRENDA *high-tails it down to the concourse.* NICK *is stunned.*]

MIRANDA

Do you know her, Uncle?

SIR JAMES

[*Distracted*] Eh? Yes ... why are the judges taking so long?

LAURIE

Too big a heart. Gave his all. Let's hope your heart can put up with this takeover, old son. [LAURIE *has forgotten the horse entirely*]

NICK

You nobbled it?

LAURIE

The horse? Not me. The trainer is trying out a new vitamin diet. It'll take the racecourse vets a few months to catch up.

MIRANDA

She's fairly sharp—but she wants to work for the National Gallery. It's a boys world. Corporate art—now that's the new frontier—money to burn.

SIR JAMES

[*Mishearing, testily*] I don't have money to burn.

LAURIE

What do you reckon if I talk to Sir Thomas myself.

NICK

I don't know. He's very different from you.

LAURIE

We have to play this really quickly, old son, or else I'm fit only for the knackers. We have to break them. Us revolutionaries are masters of creative destruction. Make an appointment for me for tomorrow.

NICK

Sunday?

LAURIE

I suppose the old geezer goes to church. [NICK *nods*] I'm a Catholic but do you see me in church? Church stops a person relating directly to God.

RACECALLER

Very distressing. Very distressing, ladies and gentlemen, to see the end of a great horse.

LAURIE

Died a winner! OK, tomorrow arvo. Then tee up a meeting with a young turk from the bank Monday evening—take him out to a long liquid lunch at the poshest restaurant—tell him I'm God, then shove him before me. OK?

RACECALLER

Protest dismissed on the sixth ladies and gentlemen. Byzantine Girl is first—

SIR JAMES

Oh, no—

LAURIE

He won!

[LAURIE *is ecstatic,* NICK *looks at his ticket and we see an elated smile cross his face.*]

RACECALLER

Unforgiven second.

SIR JAMES

[*To himself*] What now?

RACECALLER

Arwon third.

LAURIE

Touch me, Nick—I'm hot.

MIRANDA

Are you alright, Uncle?

SIR JAMES

[*Unconvincing*] Yes ... [*He exits, she follows*]

MIRANDA

[*following him*] Uncle James, are you alright?

NICK

Laurie, I'd like to talk about working for you—

LAURIE

But you are, Nick. We're going to be a team.

NICK

I couldn't—

LAURIE

Think about it, Nick. Porsche. Money. House on the harbour. [NICK *is not wilting*]

NICK

Your methods—

LAURIE

I'm no choir boy, Nick, but I have my ethics. Is that what you want, handsome young boys—you can buy ten—

NICK

[*disgusted*] No.

LAURIE

[*he notices* NICK *momentarily glancing at a woman passing by*] Into dusky beauties, eh? The best of both worlds. I see you tearing through the streets of Point Piper in your red Porsche, a beautiful brown skinned cutie sucking you off as you hurtle around corners at 200 ks an hour. [A *beat, he beams*] As many girls as you want, Nick; and you know what they say: experience is the best lecher. And you know why they'll crawl to you? Because you'll be in the Gods. Up where the decisions are made—the ones you make. I can give you fame. Wealth. Power. [*Shaking his hand*] Partner. Now where do you suppose Sir James is? If he's a desperate loser I think I know where. [*He exits*]

[NICK *broods*]

NICK

[*to himself*] He's fixed the race. Jump ship. Do it! Jump ship. [*Remembering* LAURIE's *words*] Creative destruction. Up in the Gods. [*Shaking his head*] Go back to Esko's. Mark this down to experience. [*A beat*] Boring but safe back there.

MIRANDA

Where's the arsehole?

NICK

Collecting his winnings.

MIRANDA

You involved with him?

NICK

[*embarrassed*] You must be joking.

MIRANDA

That tip he gave Uncle James—Uncle James was very depressed.

NICK

Yes, he must be. Miranda? What if I left Esko and worked for Laurie Blake.

MIRANDA

You wouldn't sell yourself that cheap.

NICK

It's like plugging into an electric circuit.

MIRANDA

Don't be stupid, Nick: you might find yourself ending up being electrocuted. I'd better find Uncle James.

[*She goes. Silence.* NICK *broods and then takes a ticket out of pocket*]

NICK

[*to himself*] Byzantine Girl ... a winner. [*A beat*] Two hundred ks an hour. [*Smiling*] Winners are grinners [*He goes.*]

The racecourse toilets. Distant sounds of the running of race seven, SIR JAMES *is standing disconsolately in the toilet block tearing up his ticket, dropping the pieces into the toilet bowl.*

SIR JAMES

Ruined ... Ruined ... but not forgiven.

[*He feels like vomiting and, getting down on his knees, vomits into the toilet bowl.* LAURIE *enters and spots him*]

LAURIE

[*ebulliently*] Sir James!

[*Because he is face down in the bowl,* SIR JAMES *does not see who is calling to him*]

SIR JAMES

Leave me alone!

LAURIE

Sorry about the tip.

SIR JAMES

I want to suicide. I feel awful.

[LAURIE *takes a piece of toilet paper and wipes* SIR JAMES' *mouth.*]

How humiliating ... how disgusting. A nadir in my life. Thank goodness my niece can't see me now.

LAURIE

Yes, thank goodness you're in the gentlemen's.

SIR JAMES

[*Recognising* LAURIE] You! You gave me the tip.

LAURIE

Unforgiven came in second. Didn't you bet for a place?

SIR JAMES

Always bet on first past the post. I was hoping that protest on Byzantine whatever would be upheld. My luck is terrible.

LAURIE

Perhaps not, Sir James.

SIR JAMES

I couldn't get lower.

LAURIE

Your luck can change. Why don't you off load your Burchett shares. I'll buy them at a good price—3.60.

SIR JAMES

I couldn't do that.

LAURIE

4.20.

SIR JAMES

Thomas is my closest friend.

LAURIE

5.00.

SIR JAMES

It would be treachery. Betrayal. Geelong Grammar boys don't do that—well, at least, not to each other. [*He feels sick again and puts his head into the bowl and vomits again.* LAURIE *slaps him on the back*] No, no!

[*Pale faced and nauseous* SIR JAMES *brings his head out of the bowl.*]

LAURIE

Four per cent is peanuts in the scheme of things.

SIR JAMES

Sir James Wilson head first down a toilet bowl in a public place.

LAURIE

I won't tell anyone. Now, about those shares.

SIR JAMES

No, I couldn't betray him.

LAURIE

He wouldn't know.

SIR JAMES

You're attempting to take over his company. He'd know I'd sold them to you.

LAURIE

Sell them to another company.

SIR JAMES

One that you control?

LAURIE

I can create a company for precisely these events.

SIR JAMES

It's illegal.

LAURIE

Not your problem. Sir Thomas would never know.

SIR JAMES

I can't be a traitor.

LAURIE

No one would know. You'd have money and no one

would know the depths you've sunk to. 5.20. Tops.

SIR JAMES

No!

[*He vomits in the howl again, then lifts up his head*]

Yes.

SCENE FOUR · THE BIRD OF PARADISE

The aviary. Late afternoon. THOMAS *is feeding his birds. Mumbling their names. There is something about the way he moves and his attitude that gives one a sense of mental wandering.*

THOMAS

[*to himself*] There is the prodigal son. The black sheep. The ungrateful son. The son of the loins, who is not your son. The son who is supposed to fill your life with warmth, but who doesn't. Son of sons. Empty sun of my loins.

[LAURIE *enters the aviary*]

LAURIE

Sir Thomas ...

THOMAS

Close the door! Close the damn door. The birds will get out!

[LAURIE *does as he is told*]

LAURIE

[*returning*] Done.

[*Silence as* THOMAS *pretends to ignore him and doesn't offer him a coat or hat*]

Nice birds ...

THOMAS

You could say that about a Bird of Paradise. [*Testily*]

Come out with it. [LAURIE *is nonplussed*] What was too important to say over the phone ...

LAURIE

As you know, Sir Thomas, my company is bidding for a major share of your company.

THOMAS

Fifty-one per cent, I hear. [*A beat*] It's all so simple. You'll put out a Part A offer and statement. I'll put out a Part B statement and in it detail what's wrong with your offer and shoot you down easily. Your humiliation will be totally public.

[*A bird shits on* LAURIE. *He tries to ignore it but* THOMAS *is amused*]

A bird doesn't like you, Blake. They're a good judge of character. I was expecting someone like you. Crude. Coarse. Out of his depth.

LAURIE

Say what you will—

THOMAS

I am. Nouveau riche. Though from what I've heard, presently nouveau without the riche.

[LAURIE *does not understand the term*]

LAURIE

What do you mean?

THOMAS

You're out of your financial depth, Blake. Tiger, Tiger burning dully.

LAURIE

Don't quite get your drift, Sir Thomas. I have come along here to ask if—

THOMAS

If I would like to buy back the shares you bought and now cannot pay for?

LAURIE

No, whether you would like to sell your shares to me.

[THOMAS *is so stunned he laughs*]

THOMAS

You have no money, I heard from Esko.

LAURIE

I have debt.

THOMAS

You're a crazy man.

LAURIE

No, I want to buy your forty per cent.

THOMAS

Get out of here, you ridiculous man. Even if you had the money, do you think I'd sell, or my son would sell? This is not a supermarket. Burchett's is the biggest brewery in the country—we own other extensive interests and they've all been part of four generations of work and family pride. You would not understand how my business is not my business, it belongs to past generations and future generations, so in another two hundred years the name Burchett will still be one of Sydney's if not Australia's most important names.

LAURIE

It'll be forgotten.

[THOMAS *cannot believe the cheek of this man.*]

THOMAS

This from a criminal!

LAURIE

This is what Australia is, Sir Thomas. A land of opportunity. You belong to the past, because the moment you start believing in the past is the moment you're fucking gone.

THOMAS

Get out. [THOMAS *is becoming agitated*] You're upsetting my birds!

LAURIE

You know what I've always thought, ever since I was young I figured it out. I've never been cowed by anyone in high position because all men piss and shit. Only some put on airs that they don't.

THOMAS

What a mind you have.

LAURIE

And I'll tell you a few other things. I bet that the first Burchett was like me. You don't make money by doing good deeds. You're finished, you belong in the mouldy past.

THOMAS

This family—

LAURIE

You've got no one left, except a son and I hear he's a fruit. He won't have children. The Burchett name is a dead end.

THOMAS

[*angrily*] Get out—I'll never sell, neither will my son. I love him, he knows that. You can go.

[LAURIE *has overplayed his hand*]

LAURIE

Look, Sir Thomas. I am actually in a bit of a bind. I can't get out without taking a financial beating and I don't seem to be able to get a majority of shares. All I want is a seat on the board.

THOMAS

I couldn't stand to see anyone as uncouth as you facing me across a board room table.

LAURIE

What the fuck does that mean?

THOMAS

You'll never understand good breeding.

LAURIE

Birds have good breeding, humans are mongrels. Sir James Wilson—

THOMAS

A good man, a good man—

LAURIE

He sold you out. He sold me his four per cent.

THOMAS

[*shocked*] He didn't—

LAURIE

'fraid so, Sir Thomas. He stabbed you in the back—not the front—too much good breeding to do that.

THOMAS

He didn't!

LAURIE

[*going for the kill*] Your company is in corporate menopause. Its dividends are pathetic. It has a bloated management and is twenty years behind the times. When I get the shares—

THOMAS

Over my dead body—

LAURIE

And I will because the shareholders will see me as a breath of fresh air—

THOMAS

I want you to leave.

LAURIE

You're a carcass of history.

THOMAS

[*calling*] Samuel—Samuel! Throw this man out!

LAURIE

NO one can hear you, Sir Thomas. You're an old man. You're a ghost already and no one can fucking hear you.

THOMAS

Samuel!

LAURIE

I'm going to get Burchetts whether you like it or not!

THOMAS

[*agitated. The birds sound terrified*] My birds. You're frightening my birds—

LAURIE

Give me the fucking shares!

THOMAS

Get out. My birds!

LAURIE

I'm fucking desperate old man, give them to me!

[THOMAS *collapses on the floor of the cage. Victim of a heart attack*]

Shit ...

[*He touches the supine* THOMAS *with his foot confirming that* THOMAS *is dead*]

Great ... [*To noisy birds*] Shut up! [*The aviary is suddenly quiet. To himself*] Got to think ... how am I going to get those shares. His son's got twenty per cent ... has he willed his twenty to him? Probably left it to some fucking lost homing pigeons' club. Got to spend money to make money. Got to strike while the iron's hot, Laurie. You don't have much time.

SCENE FIVE · THE BRIDGE OF DREAMS

LAURIE's *office. Night. It overlooks the city of Sydney.* MIRANDA *is setting up her projection equipment. From the other room there is the constant ringing of telephones.* NICK, *nicely tipsy from a long lunch, enters with* SIMON MACKENZIE, *a banker. They bring in a bottle of wine and two glasses.*

NICK

The future of banking is in the hands of people like yourself, Simon. Only bankers like yourself—

[*Both* MIRANDA *and* NICK *are astonished to see each other, but are extremely confident*]

Miranda—what a surprise.

MIRANDA

Laurie is paying through the nose for my expertise. What about you?

NICK

Porsche. Penthouse apartment. Penthouse Pet of the year. Everything's happened so quickly. Like being struck by lightning.

SIMON

A bit heady up here. The lights. The harbour.

NICK

We're in the gods. It's so high up, when it's raining on the peasants in the street, it's sunny up here.

[*Suddenly* LAURIE *enters, beaming and bright, carrying three cans of Burchett's beer*]

LAURIE

No wine drinking in my office. [*Throwing cans at* NICK *and* SIMON *who have to catch them with one hand, while clutching their wine glass with the other*] Remember—we're taking over Burchett's beer.

NICK

Laurie, this is Simon MacKenzie, ANZ Head of Investment and Banking.

LAURIE

Ah, Simon. [*Shaking hands*] Lovely to see you. Nick been looking after you?

SIMON

Yes, we had a great lunch. A long one.

LAURIE

That's the spirit! No doubt Nick's filled you in about what we want to talk about.

MIRANDA

Do you want me to go?

LAURIE

No, I paid you to show me the slides, so show them to me.

MIRANDA

I'll have to turn off the lights.

[*She does so*]

LAURIE

[*to* SIMON] We can see the lights of Sydney better that way.

[*The lights go off*]

Hey, Simon. Nick. Put your hands in my trouser pockets. [*They are reluctant*] Go on, one hand in other pocket. Beware the python. Nah, come on. Put your hands in my pockets. [*Both men gingerly put a hand in either pocket*] What do you feel? [*They are puzzled*]

SIMON

Don't know, Laurie.

NICK

Don't know.

[*He takes their hands out*]

LAURIE

You know what's in my pockets? Reality! [*He takes a handful of barley out of each pocket*] This is the reality that creates beer. Barley! I bought some on the way here. [*To* SIMON] To remind you that I'm buying reality. Real things that grow. Enough of playing with my nuts. [*To* MIRANDA] Start. I'm watching. [*To* SIMON] We can watch the light show in here. The lights of Sydney—only it's more cultured in here. You went to university?

SIMON

In Victoria.

LAURIE

We're up so high here you can see all the way to the Melbourne Club. Some sensible men down south. Like Elliot. God, if I had a money box as big as his nose I'd be a millionaire.

[*They both laugh. The image on the wall is an Australian painting by Eugene Von Guerard.*]

MIRANDA

This is a painting by Eugene Von Guerard. [*She starts to explain it and the period.* LAURIE *turns back to* SIMON *and whispers to him*]

LAURIE

[*whispering*] Like to be up her, eh? You ever felt the orgasm?

SIMON

[*not getting the drift*] What?

LAURIE

The rush. Like fucking the sexiest girl in the world. You wouldn't have felt it, Simon. Not just yet. Making a deal, a big deal is like the best orgasm.

SIMON

In a state bank—

LAURIE

Deregulation coming in. Imagine the amount you could earn. You yourself. Get it into your noggin, Simon. A commission on selling a house—a wolf whistle at a pretty sheila. Commission on selling a row of townhouses—foreplay. A factory—a knee trembler. Commission for arranging a loan for millions of dollars: wild orgasm with your favourite movie star.

SIMON

You want a lot of money.

LAURIE

Because I think big. Your bank stands to earn a lot. Just think of the interest it'll earn and your prestige at that amount of interest. Your commission. New car. Cars.

Porsche. BMW. Couple of town houses on Lavender Bay—look, you can see them from here. Playmate of the Year—'cos Nick has cornered the Penthouse market. You'll be the golden boy. The one who says, 'I know how the new economy works. And it does work'.

MIRANDA

Louis Buvelot's paintings in recent times—I feel I could be talking to no one. Do you want me to go?

LAURIE

No, no, no. I want you to earn your money.

[MIRANDA *shakes her head and goes on to a Tom Roberts, explaining it loudly, having given up.* LAURIE *occasionally glances at the slides as, wanting to be out of here,* MIRANDA *rushes through them as quickly as possible believing she is in the presence of a philistine.*]

So what do you think, Simon?

SIMON

The interest is attractive.

LAURIE

It's more than attractive. It's a sexy rate.

SIMON

[*becoming excited*] It's a risk.

LAURIE

And you know that we'll be able to sell off a lot of assets to pay you. Look, Simon. Look out there. There are hundreds of large businesses and most of them are run badly. Nick and I will come in with our team and make Burchett's brewery not only sell more beer but reach out into the world. It needs ideas. Imagination. Nick and I have got both. And you, well, with your bank's involvement, you and your bank stand to be at the forefront of this new empire.

SIMON

It's a lot of money.

LAURIE

When I was ten, a penny was a lot of money. When I was twenty, a hundred dollars was a lot of money, well, now, money is relative. This bridging loan is unique—we call it the Bridge of Dreams loan.

SIMON

The profits for the bank could be enormous.

LAURIE

Think sex. Think money. And you know what money is? Money is the root of all women.

MIRANDA

This Arthur Boyd is from the half caste bride series. Here the two men play cards to see who gets her.

[NICK *swings his head to see the image,* LAURIE *is concentrating on stroking* SIMON]

LAURIE

Get the papers ready tomorrow morning, Simon. A bridge of dreams.

SIMON

We're on the threshold of a new way of financial borrowing.

LAURIE

You've seen the future, Simon, and you know what that future is: me! [*A beat. Big smile*] And you.

SIMON

You've made me feel anything's possible, Laurie. Bye. [*To* NICK] Next time lunch is on me.

LAURIE

[*as* SIMON *goes*] On the way out ask my secretary for a free TV.

NICK

[*happily*] We got it!

LAURIE

The money but still not the shares. Old Burchett made a will passing them all on to his son. We've got to win him tomorrow. I've been finding out a bit about his son. Economics is psychology, Nick. Find the weaknesses. Burchett's son is a pillow biter. [*About* MIRANDA] I'd be up her like a rat up a drainpipe.

[MIRANDA *overhears and is angry, but cool*]

MIRANDA

I'm a very expensive drainpipe, Mr Blake and I have a grating to keep the rats out. And what's the point of me showing you these slides, you weren't listening.

LAURIE

Throw up a slide. Any slide. Go on. [*She projects a Fred Williams*] Fred Williams. You yangs. Another one. [*She throws up a Sali Herman*] Sali Herman, Sydney artist. [*Clicking his fingers*] More! [*He recognises each one*] Boyd, Arthur. Tom Roberts. Rupert Bunny. Eric Gill. Brett Whiteley. Louis Buvelot.

[*It is an impressive display of his mental retention and* MIRANDA *is impressed*]

Well?

[MIRANDA *is impressed, but tries not to show it*]

NICK

I'm going home. I think I've passed from tipsy to pissed.

LAURIE

Tomorrow afternoon for the pillow biter.

NICK

Yep. I'll be there. Time to push the Porsche through its paces.

LAURIE

Yeh, and give your Pet one for me.

[NICK *leaves*]

[*Pause.*]

MIRANDA

I might go home too.

LAURIE

I still have to know about Abo art. Remember, you didn't come cheap.

MIRANDA

My knowledge is an expensive thing.

[*She goes to another box of slides*]

Why do you want to know all this?

LAURIE

Because I'm a glutton for beautiful things.

[*He moves towards her speaking quietly, almost whis-*

pering. She seems caught in the glare of the slide, as if mesmerised by the light]

LAURIE

Butchers are always happy. Have you noticed that? Women are happy when they visit a butcher. [*He grabs her and starts to undress her*] They imagine him undressing her. Because he knows flesh so well. The muscles, the soft underbelly, and he can be so tender to the insides. [*Placing his hand over her rib cage*] She knows, can feel the hand that has put a knife between the ribs, but has also felt it, tenderly like this. Butchers are the only men who know how easily flesh bruises. And he places her on the chopping block and she hears herself landing there, like a flat slap, like the slap of a piece of soft, tender, steak slice. Because they know what it is to slaughter, they know the body better than anyone. Now, I'm going to fuck you like a butcher.

SCENE SIX · TROUBLE IN PARADISE

BRENDA *is in a swim suit, sunning herself on a deck chair, sipping champagne. In the background dogs are barking. She notices something happening in the garden.*

BRENDA

[*yelling*] No, prune the shrubs, don't bloody cut them down. Listen to me. [*Illustrating*] Prune, don't axe them down. [*To herself*] Bloody Vietnamese, probably never seen anything else other than a market garden.

[LAURIE *comes out, wearing a business suit*]

Where you going? Meryl and Ed are coming around.

LAURIE

I have to go to a meeting.

BRENDA

A root more likely. [*He sighs, exasperated*] It's how you used to like me talking in bed. [*A beat*] You got in at three this morning.

LAURIE

I was preparing for the meeting with Burchett.

BRENDA

Don't ever, ever let me catch you with anyone, Laurie. By, god, I'll cut it off.

LAURIE

[*noticing gardeners*] How many gardeners have we got now?

BRENDA

Four.

LAURIE

I can't pay for them. We're cutting things pretty fine as it is, Brenda. Fire them!

BRENDA

They're one family. Four Vietnamese for the price of one. They're pathetically grateful for a job.

LAURIE

What are they going to do—plant rice paddies? We should keep the dogs indoors.

BRENDA

What's the matter with you. You seem toey.

LAURIE

You take everything for granted. What would happen if it all went.

BRENDA

I wouldn't care.

LAURIE

You would.

BRENDA

No, I wouldn't.

LAURIE

Back to me driving trucks?

BRENDA

We spent time together then. Not now. I'd sooner go back to living in the garage when we first started out. You were romantic then. Remember after we first met you were broke and you sent me two dozen roses with 'I love you, Brenda' written on the back of the bill.

LAURIE

Christ, champagne in the morning.

BRENDA

It gives me something to do. Darling, I wouldn't care if we had to start over again.

LAURIE

I haven't got where I am to start over again, Brenda.

BRENDA

You really are in trouble, aren't you?

LAURIE

[*agitated*] I've got to win him over. I've used all my money to buy the shares. I've leased the top floor of the most expensive building in Australia to impress the bloody bankers. If I sell the shares, I sell at a loss. I've got to buy him out.

BRENDA

Laurie—I want you to listen to me. You know what we are—lucky! You come from the working class. So do I. Don't you understand—you're taking on the establishment. Burchett's are bluebloods. They're as close as thieves. Be what we are, Laurie. Leave it at this. Look at it—never in our wildest dreams did we imagine having this.

LAURIE

I can't stop. They want me to give in. They want to beat me. They think I'm stupid. Not one of them. But I'll show them. They think they know it all. I'll show them that someone like me can take them on and win.

BRENDA

They're as thick as thieves, Laurie, They'll freeze you out.

LAURIE

I don't care, because if I beat them, they'll no longer be relevant.

[*The portable phone rings,* BRENDA *answers it. The dogs bark,* LAURIE, *lost in thought, notices the gardeners.*]

No, no, no! It's oleander. Don't wipe it in your eyes, it's poison. [*Calling out*] Agent orange! Agent orange! [*to himself*] Fred Williams, Ian Fairweather, Lambert, must remember fucking Lambert. Christ, I feel like I'm sitting for an exam.

BRENDA

[*shaken*] Nick's in hospital.

LAURIE

What?

BRENDA

He rammed his Porsche into a telephone pole last night. Blind drunk. He's in a very bad way. Broken ribs, broken legs. He's touch and go.

LAURIE

I need him! He was supposed to be with me today. He did that deliberately.

BRENDA

Laurie, listen to yourself.

LAURIE

He did it deliberately. Couldn't take the strain. He deliberately crashed his car. I'll sue him for careless driving. [*Angry and apprehensive, the dogs are barking more loudly.*] Don't touch the hysteria. Leave the hysteria alone. Touch my dogs and I'll ship you back to Vietnam. [*He goes*]

[BRENDA *shakes her head and pours herself another champagne*]

BRENDA

[*sipping it*] Ah ... luscious. [*To herself*] Where would I go? An old chook. Lonely to boot. I'd miss the champagne. He cares more for his dogs than me. [*Yelling at the gardeners*] For crying out loud—leave the bloody Wisteria alone.

SCENE SEVEN · THE GOOD SON

The enormous living room of TERRY BURCHETT, LAURIE *enters with* TERRY. *Day.* TERRY *is carrying a bottle of champagne under one arm, both he and* LAURIE *are sipping from their glasses of champagne.*

LAURIE

[*impressed*] The living room's as big as a footie ground.

TERRY

Yes, it is large, isn't it? It was once a ballroom when the Macleans owned it. He made a fortune in silver. Then spent it all.

LAURIE

Like an art gallery.

TERRY

[*condescendingly*] They're famous Australian paintings—I know why you're here.

[LAURIE *is nervous,* TERRY *seems confident and cheerful almost and is the perfect host.*]

LAURIE

I just wanted to talk to you. To get the lie of the land. Love the Streeton. Good example. Now those Sali Herman—not quite in fashion now, but he will be. [*Taking more champagne*] Ta. [*He heads around the room*] A beautiful Williams. Beautiful. He taught us to see landscape again.

TERRY

Yes, he did, Laurie, yes, he did.

LAURIE

I've always adored Australian art—even before it became fashionable, so when I heard you had a collection I thought I might take a squizz—

TERRY

And try to get me to sell my shares.

LAURIE

[*laughing apprehensively*] This is your crowning achievement. The paintings are superb but these burial poles. York Peninsula, I'd say.

TERRY

[*enthusiastically*] Early Groote Eylandt.

LAURIE

Yes, yes. The aborigines ... that's what makes it great art. Four thousand years of practice makes perfect.

TERRY

If I don't give you the shares you're probably done for, aren't you, Laurie?

LAURIE

Christ, no.

TERRY

It's surprising how many businessmen are what you'd call poofters, Laurie. You learn a lot at dunnies.

[LAURIE *seems caught a few steps behind*]

LAURIE

[trying *to make joke of it*] Maybe I should hang out there.

TERRY

As rough trade? [*A beat*] Without my shares it'll probably be back to driving blood and bone and all this art knowledge would be for zilch. You're perspiring.

LAURIE

Arthur Boyd's *Half-Caste.*

TERRY

If I sell them to you. I sell away our past.

LAURIE

I understand quite perfectly. [A *beat, staring at paintings*] A nice Lambert.

TERRY

My grandparents. He painted them several times.

LAURIE

Your collection is magnificent.

TERRY

Every room. I'm going to have to build a storeroom.

LAURIE

Almost a full time job to look after them.

TERRY

I have a few staff. Not many though.

LAURIE

So you're going to give collecting up?

TERRY

What makes you say that?

LAURIE

To run the business. It went downhill the last couple of years. It's going to take all your energy to put it back on its feet.

TERRY

I haven't given a lot of thought to it—Father dear is just dead.

LAURIE

Died at my feet.

TERRY

Covered in bird shit, I hear. Or did you shit on him? I know people into such practices. He must have loved me—he gave me the shares.

LAURIE

He did love you. He just couldn't put it into words. You know men of that generation. Giving you the shares was his way of saying that.

TERRY

I guess you could interpret it that way.

[*Pause.* LAURIE *is making little headway*]

LAURIE

What other way would you interpret it?

TERRY

I have no idea, except for the obvious: he wanted a Burchett to be in control of The Empire. Me. In control of the brewery, newspaper, hop fields. [*Enjoying this*] But how am I going to give birth through my arse, Laurie?

LAURIE

People call me crude ...

TERRY

Hard to imagine my father saying it, but he did. To reinforce the fact that I was a Burchett genetic dead end. They didn't want me to be part of the family—their rituals and ceremonies of family life. Now, at the last moment, I was the lifebuoy for the name, so he threw me his shares. A moment's gesture to make up for a lifetime of injury. You don't know what's happening, do you?

LAURIE

I came to talk, to see your paintings—

TERRY

I admire your immersion in Australian art history, Laurie. I heard through the grapevine that Miranda Wilson gave you a crash course. She helped choose some of mine. So we do have something in common.

LAURIE

I'm at a bit of a loss. I came here—

TERRY

Don't you understand, Laurie. It didn't matter, doesn't matter, what you do—you've lucked in.
[A *pause,* TERRY *enjoying* LAURIE'S *momentary confusion*]
You know how it goes. The first generation builds up the empire, the second extends and consolidates it and the third, generally a cocksucker, spends it all. [*A beat*] I'll build that storehouse, twice the size. I have children, you know. Here, on the walls. [*A beat*] I'm going to call my financial adviser, tell him to sell the shares to you. It's all

yours. [*Smiling*] I have waited years to revenge myself on that arsehole that was my father. You understand now? You have lucked in. Another good son would have told you to fuck off. Champagne? [LAURIE *nods, dazed,* TERRY *is about to head off, but stops*] what about the name. Burchett brewery?

LAURIE

I'll keep it.

TERRY

Like hell you will. Obliterate it. You know what a family is, Laurie. Singularly they're sane, collectively it's a psychopath.

LAURIE

And that's the reason you're giving it to me?

TERRY

I want to set the cat amongst the pigeons.

[TERRY *goes to make the call:* LAURIE *can hardly believe his luck. He wriggles with excitement*]

LAURIE

[*to himself*] You did it, Laurie ....you did it ... You took them on and won ...

[*He holds up his arms in victory, there is applause,* LAURIE *takes imaginary microphone and addresses his audience*]

Thank you. Thank you. Now tonight is going to be a great night. Blake Industries is now one of the largest conglomerates in Australia. Many of you haven't met—the pace has been so quick. So read the name tags of those opposite and get to know your business mate. And also get to know someone else.

[*He looks to the wings and waves somebody out. It is Dave Ulmer, wearing his footie gear*]

Ladies and gentlemen. Dave Ulmer, Captain of the Falcons. From an hour ago, Blake Industries now owns the Falcons. [*Putting arm around Ulmer*] Why the Falcons? Bottom of the league for years, but I've always supported them. And like me they'll take on the bluebloods with their lawyers, knights and private schools and win!

[*Wild cheers. Dave Ulmer exits*]

The future belongs to Blake Industries.

[*More cheers. Singing*]

The world is bright and new
everything's there for the take
every mine has a golden seam
you owe it all to Blakey's dream.

Everything not nailed down
is there for you to take
every day you'll reign supreme
living example of Blakey's Dream.

The future is what you'll make it
we're not about to go and break it
And you know what we're gonna do
We'll take on the world and Blake it!

ACT TWO

SCENE ONE · GREENMAIL

LAURIE'S *office. Day.* LAURIE *and* MIRANDA, *who is handing him postcards, a pile of art books and catalogues nearby.*

MIRANDA

From the whole auction the best examples will be a Corot, a Jacques-Louis David, a De Kooning, a Monet and Francis Bacon.

LAURIE

What do you think?

MIRANDA

The Corot is not a good example of his work and the De Kooning is one of his later examples: his Alzheimers phase. The Monet is wonderful. Waterlilies.

LAURIE

Buy that then.

MIRANDA

It'll cost a fortune. I've heard through the grapevine that Freddie Arrow is going to bid for it—he'll push the price up.

LAURIE

Freddie Arrow's a pom ... let's give him a run for his money. If we buy it—what will it mean for Blake Art Galleries?

MIRANDA

The world will sit up and take notice.

[*They both smile at the thought*]

LAURIE

We'll be on our way—

MIRANDA

To becoming the largest private gallery in the world.

LAURIE

I feel like Adam. You know, naming everything. Blake's Beer. Blake's Trucks, Blake's Art Galleries, Blake's Constructions.

INTERCOM

Mr Blake, Mr Simon MacKenzie is on the phone again—he says it's urgent.

LAURIE

Tell him I'm busy.

INTERCOM

Yes, Mr Blake.

[*A distant alarm sounds*]

MIRANDA

The security alarm. Why do you have it?

LAURIE

Need to, some nuts keep on threatening me because they lost their jobs in the Burchett sell off and reorganisation. Now, like *The Telegraph* said about me this morning: Laurie Blake is Refreshing. Be refreshed all the time, stick around, kid.

[*Pause. The alarm is still going*]

I wish they'd shut that bloody thing off.

MIRANDA

What do you mean by stick around?

LAURIE

Precisely that.

MIRANDA

[*they are now shouting over the noise of the alarm*] Laurie, you're a married man.

LAURIE

In name only.

MIRANDA

You have a daughter.

LAURIE

Helen's fourteen, she can look after herself. [*About the alarm*] That's it, someone's going to be fired! [*He is about to go to the door when in walks* NICK *on crutches*]

LAURIE

Nick! [*The alarm stops*]

NICK

Sorry, I set off the security alarm. They put my bones back together with metal plates.

[*Pause*]

My job still here?

[LAURIE *is unsure,* NICK *seems physically awkward and has a strange gleam in his eyes.*]

LAURIE

Jeez, Nick, do you think you're up to it.

NICK

Quite literally, Laurie, I'm an iron man.

LAURIE

Sorry, I didn't visit you in hospital, Nick. Everyday something seemed to crop up. The Burchett deal. The unions. Fuck, it costs a lot to pay off unions nowadays. [*A beat*] But Miranda took you my pressies and stuff?

NICK

[*to* MIRANDA] Yeh, thanks. Hospital was good for me. I was busy doing therapy and doing a lot of thinking. A lot of thinking.

LAURIE

Good. Tomorrow night, I'm Australian of the Year. I'll sit you down front. You'll be on TV. I'll give you a new Porsche with special pedals.

NICK

I'm not after charity. I want to be part of everything again. [NICK *throws off his crutches and collapses deliberately onto the floor*]

LAURIE

You all right?

NICK

Pay no attention. [*He starts to move across the floor, pushing his way forward on his elbows*] I found at physio classes that I could only think when I moved. [*He moves across the floor like a snake*]

LAURIE

Gives me the creeps, Nick.

NICK

Pay no attention, I said. This injury did me a world of good, Laurie. I was in so much pain that even morphine couldn't stop me from screaming. The only way to conquer the pain was to think—to think of schemes and deals. The pain made me concentrate. In my head is an explosion of ideas. Give me a problem. Go on, give me a problem.

LAURIE

Well, everything's pretty OK at the moment. Though Simon Mackenzie's been at me because I'm a bit behind in interest payments after buying more of *The Herald*. Then the other day I was a bit pissed and bought nine per cent of BHP. I need to sell off some assets quickly.

NICK

BHP? [*Astonished*] You bought into BHP?

LAURIE

Yeh, should never buy shares when I'm pissed. Bought in too high. Could never get a controlling interest. Besides it's out of my range. And bloody Simon—

NICK

Pay no attention to Simon.

LAURIE

He's ringing me up every half hour. They're going to lose a fortune if we don't come through.

NICK

It's the bank's problem, not ours. A thousand dollar debt is our problem, a 100 million debt is theirs. Squeeze him—ask for more.

LAURIE

More? Are you on some kind of medication.

NICK

I'm on a natural high, Laurie. The more debt we have, the more the banks have to give us in the hope we can buy companies so that we can sell off their assets to pay back the bank. It's brilliant but brutal in its simplicity.

[LAURIE *is mesmerised by* NICK *crawling across the floor, his mind working overtime*]

Also it's important to keep debt, no matter how artificial it is. All interest payments on debt are fully tax deductible. OK, the next thing. We put all the companies off shore. Cook Islands. Places like that. No tax need be paid here in Australia—or anywhere, really.

LAURIE

Jeez, Nick, I don't know if they put a metal plate in your scone or not, but you're firing on all cylinders.

NICK

My mind is what you've got, Laurie. My body is useless.

LAURIE

Instead of screwing girls, you'll screw companies.

NICK

My life for Blake Enterprises. As everyone here should give their lives. Ever noticed that every Thursday the staff dash out to deposit their pay checks? Pay them late Fridays after the banks are closed. And we can keep the extra interest accumulated over the weekend.

INTERCOM

Mr Blake, it's Mr Simon MacKenzie on the phone again.

LAURIE

Tell him I'm in a meeting.

NICK

No, Laurie, let me at him. I know his type: swot at his State school, pass degree in Commerce at Deakin Uni. Piece of cake.

LAURIE

Mia, put him through.

[*The telephone call is put through over the loud speaker*]

NICK

Hello? Simon ...

SIMON

Laurie—boy, am I glad to get through to you.

NICK

This is Nick Albert here, Simon.

SIMON

Nick, I thought you were in hospital.

NICK

Yeh, well, I'm back. What do you want?

SIMON

Management is worried sick—we want our money—

NICK

Yes, Laurie knows you want your money. Blake Investments is finding it hard to flog some of the Burchett assets. What Laurie needs is some really good assets—some prime companies. Like more of BHP.

SIMON

You're crazy—no person in their right mind would give him more money—

NICK

But you will, Simon—it's the only way to solve your problem.

SIMON

The board is starting to ask questions.

NICK

Listen you fuckin' coward—You are going to be crucified.

LAURIE

[*horrified*] Nick!

[NICK *waves* LAURIE *to be quiet*]

NICK

The only way to save yourself is to give us another bridging loan. Another Bridge of Dreams. We want half a billion. I said, have you balls, or are you a sissy?

SIMON

Nick—don't be like this. This is a crisis. I thought you were my friend.

NICK

A friend is just a potential enemy. This afternoon. And if you don't fucking come through you are history, mate. You're a has been at twenty-five if you don't give us the money. Bye, Simon. Hang up, Mia. [*Smiling at astonished* MIRANDA *and* LAURIE] I call it phone terrorism.

[LAURIE *looks across to* MIRANDA *who is smiling*]

LAURIE

What do you reckon?

MIRANDA

He'll come through. He needs you.

INTERCOM

Mr Blake—Mr Barry Saint John [*She pronounces it as sinjin*] would like to speak to you.

[*The three exchange glances—this is an important name*]

LAURIE

[*To* NICK] Saint John ...

NICK

Is he in town? [*A beat*] He's your only competition now, Laurie.

MIRANDA

If he's calling you, he wants something.

LAURIE

Mia—put him through.

ST JOHN

This is Barry Saint John.

LAURIE

Hi, Barry.

ST JOHN

I wonder if it's convenient for you to have a chat this afternoon. Perhaps three.

[LAURIE *looks to* NICK *who holds up five fingers*]

LAURIE

Bit busy around then—say five o'clock.

NICK

[*to* LAURIE] Here.

LAURIE

My office.

ST JOHN

My penthouse.

LAURIE

See you then.

ST JOHN

Excellent.

[*Pause*]

NICK

Could be important, Laurie.

LAURIE

The only one who's got more than me.

NICK

Crush him, Laurie.

MIRANDA

It's sort of like war all of this, isn't it?

LAURIE

Yeh, and you're the spoils of victory.

MIRANDA

Speaking of spoils, I'd better head off to the auction rooms.

LAURIE

Yeh, let's have the world sit up and take notice.

[LAURIE *gives her a peck on the cheek,* NICK *gobbles down some pills from a bottle.*]

MIRANDA

Bye, darling. Bye, Nick.

NICK

[*mouth full*] Bye.

MIRANDA

[*happily to* LAURIE] It's sort of like being part of the Three Musketeers. [*She heads out*]

LAURIE

She's a marvel running the gallery. You know what she said to me the other day, Nick? 'The reason I went for you, Laurie, is that you're the only man who ever said to me, "I'm going to fuck you so hard and long you'll forget what it's like to be vertical"'. [NICK *takes another mouthful of pills.*] Can you beat that? You alright?

NICK

Yeh, these pills are great. I got them from a debarred doctor up in the Cross. Are you serious about going for more of BHP? Greenmail them. It's like blackmail only it earns you more. Let BHP know you've bought it, they'll be so shit scared that you want to take them over they'll offer you double to sell your shares back to them.

LAURIE

[*excited*] All I have to do is say, 'Boo!'.

NICK

That's all. You understand what I'm saying, Laurie.

There's a whole universe of possibilities out there and you know what the rules are: there are no rules.

[LAURIE *looks admiringly at* NICK *who is sitting on the floor*]

SCENE TWO · SAINT JOHN

A penthouse. Day. But only the thin shivers of light shine in through Venetian blinds, SAINT JOHN *stands sipping a whiskey, wearing sunglasses,* LORNA, *his wife stands nearby. A knock on the door. He hurriedly downs his whiskey and gives the glass to* LORNA.

ST JOHN

Yes? Come in.

[LAURIE *enters*]

Mr Blake.

LAURIE

[*shaking hands*] Glad to meet you, Saint John.

LORNA

It's Saint John. [*She pronounces it 'singin'*]

LAURIE

You New Zealanders have a funny way of spelling things. Shall I just call you Barry?

ST JOHN

If you like. My wife, Lorna.

LAURIE

G'day, Lorna.

ST JOHN

A drink. I have some whiskey here. [*pouring some*]

LORNA

I was just reading about you in *The Herald.*

LAURIE

[*pleased*] I tell them not to write about me too much, after all it is my paper.

LORNA

I admire the way you give your staff editorial independence. Like the article this morning on the infamous Romanian regime.

LAURIE

Infamous? I haven't read it yet.

LORNA

I gather you have dealings with the Romanians.

LAURIE

[*shrugging*] Funny buggers—but they're OK. [A *beat*] Bit dark in here.

LORNA

Barry's very sensitive to light.

LAURIE

Is that why you're never photographed?

ST JOHN

[*Giving him whiskey*] I think like the New Guineans. Once you're photographed your soul is taken. [*A beat*] mystery is very important, isn't it?

LAURIE

I like to take things front on.

[LAURIE *pauses waiting for* SAINT JOHN *to get a drink*]

LORNA

Barry doesn't drink. He thinks important matters should be decided with a clear head.

LAURIE

What's on your mind, Baz?

[SAINT JOHN *flinches at the nickname but continues*]

ST JOHN

New Zealand became too small for me, just as Australia will eventually become too small for the both of us. I like chess, do you, Laurie?

LAURIE

Never had the time for it. Quite good at draughts at school.

[SAINT JOHN *laughs thinking* LAURIE *is joking*]

ST JOHN

You were the lovable larrikin then?

LAURIE

All depends. If someone wanted to put me down, I would react. I had a teacher who hated me and I stood up in class one day and said to him, 'One day I will buy people like you'. And I did. He's working in one of my storerooms.

ST JOHN

[*A beat*] You're after BHP?

LAURIE

[*surprised*] Who told you?

ST JOHN

Small movement in their shares. You already have nine per cent. Any more and you'll have to formally announce a takeover.

LAURIE

You're moving in too?

ST JOHN

It's the big one. It would seem natural that the biggest fish in the pond—you and I, Laurie, would take it. Or are you in it only for the greenmail?

LAURIE

I'm open to anything. [*Hiding the enormity of the deal*] It's big.

ST JOHN

The biggest. It's everything. Steel. Mining. Manufacturing, you name it.

LAURIE

Why are you telling me this?

ST JOHN

Even with your resources you can't get it.

LORNA

Alone Barry doesn't have the resources but some banks are prepared to loan him half. You can supply the other half.

ST JOHN

If you own BHP—

LAURIE

You own Australia.

ST JOHN

In a manner of speaking.

LAURIE

I could get the money on my own.

LORNA

Barry has made inquiries. Discreet, of course.

ST JOHN

I realise that. Why don't you let me start the ball rolling. I'll make the opening moves of the gambit. The board is slow and old, they won't know what hit them. I'll buy three hundred million shares. Panic will set in. You should be free by then to concentrate on buying the rest to get to fifty percent.

LAURIE

What happens then?

ST JOHN

We take over.

LAURIE

As a team?

ST JOHN

There may be the occasion when you or I buy each other out, but I think we can get on.

LAURIE

OK. A deal.

[*They shake hands*]

ST JOHN

To the largest takeover in Australia's history.

LAURIE

To history.

ST JOHN

I hear you've Australian of the year. Congratulations.

LAURIE

[*pleased as punch*] Tomorrow night. [*A beat*] See ya, Baz. Loma.

[LAURIE *goes.* LORNA *pours barry a glass of whiskey.*]

LORNA

Uncouth as you thought?

ST JOHN

You know how Australians play the professional larrikin. I just don't know how shrewd he is.

LORNA

He must have been to get where he is.

ST JOHN

The way the banks are throwing around money, anyone could walk off the street and get a million. It's like the gold rush, only the banks are the seams of gold.

LORNA

Do you think he will go with you?

ST JOHN

I think so. I don't think he truly understands what's afoot though. [*A beat*]

LORNA

He's like a boy in a lolly shop.

SCENE THREE · THE CENTRE OF THE WORLD

The pandora restaurant. Night, LAURIE *enters, looking at a postcard, he is wearing a suit, but one of his trouser legs is cut off above the knee and one of his suit sleeves is cut off at the shoulder,* HENRY, *the maître d' is escorting him.*

HENRY

Your window table, sir.

LAURIE

Thanks, Henry. [*Looking around*] There's Adam Lee from Bergin Constructions. Send over a bottle of Dom to him with the note 'How about us building the biggest office tower in the Southern Hemisphere, you old cocksucker—Blakey'.

HENRY

Very good, sir.

LAURIE

And tell that cunt to get over here.

HENRY

Which one is that, sir?

LAURIE

That cunt who edits *The Herald.* His office is just down the road. I want him here quick smart.

HENRY

Very good.

LAURIE

And some daks. [*Pointing*] Ask the guy over near the pillar. Offer him five hundred for his suit.

[HENRY *exits as* MIRANDA, *looking marvellous and very happy, enters*]

Did we get it?

MIRANDA

[*about the suit*] What happened?

LAURIE

Eh? [*Noticing*] Bloody Brenda. I get home and she's taken scissors to all my clothes. It must be the onset of menopause. [*On to what he is really interested in*] Did we get it?

MIRANDA

Yes. Christie's confirmed. I had to go way over the reserve.

LAURIE

Stiff.

MIRANDA

We have the best Monet in the world.

LAURIE

Freddie Arrow bid for it?

MIRANDA

He was desperate.

LAURIE

It's always good when you beat a pom. Especially someone as famous as Freddie Arrow. Fucking public galleries will be spewing too, eh?

[HENRY *enters with the champagne*]

I'll look after it, Henry, [HENRY *goes,* LAURIE *starts to uncork the champagne*] more dom is sold here than any liquor outlet in Australia. Pandora's is the centre of the world. Now that I'm the boss of Pandora's it's going to have a fire going even in summer.

MIRANDA

Why?

LAURIE

[*picking up crystal goblet*] Watch. [*He throws the goblet into the fire, there is a loud explosion*] Fantastic, eh? Czech crystal makes the best bang. You have a go. Go on!

[*She throws it. A satisfying bang*]

Twenty dollars a pop, but who cares—it's the bang!

[NICK *enters on steel crutches.* LAURIE *takes* nick *aside*]

[*Showing him postcard*] I bought it.

NICK

A postcard?

LAURIE

No, you drongo, the fucking Monet.

NICK

Don't know me Monet from me money, Laurie.

LAURIE

[*to* MIRANDA] I want it in my office tomorrow.

MIRANDA

I'll fly it in from L.A. [*She uses a mobile phone to call* LA.]

LAURIE

Look at that beauty in the corner, exactly like Miranda only younger.

NICK

You said it was about Saint John.

LAURIE

He wants to be my friend. Trust him?

NICK

I don't trust anyone, Laurie.

LAURIE

That's why I like you. Saint John knew about our push into BHP.

NICK

He must be interested in it.

LAURIE

I'll say, he wants a co-deal. He's promised to deliver three hundred million shares by June 30. We'll have to match him.

NICK

I thought you wanted to greenmail BHP.

LAURIE

Yeh, but this could be our chance to get half of it.

NICK

Doesn't smell right. I reckon he's already got a lot of those shares.

LAURIE

But what is he doing.

NICK

He's a real schemer, Laurie.

[NICK *falls to the ground and starts crawling, immersed in thought.* HENRY *steps over him pretending not to notice this.*]

LAURIE

I can't take you anywhere. This is a restaurant.

NICK

I told you, it's the only way I can think. Get me a Dom.

[LAURIE *clicks his fingers at* HENRY *and motions to* NICK, HENRY *understands*]

I know! I know what he's doing. He doesn't have a lot of money, in fact he's financially stressed buying into Columbia Pictures. What he's done is buy most of the shares and he's gambling that over the next month the price will fall. So he'll sell now and buy them back at a lower price and therefore make a huge profit.

[HENRY *gives* NICK *his champagne, he takes a quick sip.*]

HENRY

The cunt is on his way, sir.

LAURIE

Thanks, Henry.

[HENRY *goes. After a sip,* NICK *quickly and eagerly downs the whole glass. It refreshes him, he gets straight back to the topic as if there has been no interruption*]

NICK

But in buying them back, he'll send the price up and you'll have to buy at a price much higher than him. Two things will happen: he'll have the profit money—

LAURIE

To buy into more of BHP.

NICK

And he'll gamble on the fact that we're financially strung out in buying our quota of the shares and—

LAURIE

We'll want to get out at a lower price—

NICK

And he'll buy them at a dirt cheap price and have a majority of BHP.

LAURIE

Game, set and match.

[NICK *clicks his fingers for more champagne,* HENRY *enters, but* MIRANDA, *intrigued by all of this, comes over and pours some champagne for* NICK, *who winks at her, and gulps it eagerly.*]

HENRY

[*entering*] He won't sell his suit, Mr Blake.

LAURIE

I only take no for an answer when it's a yes. Offer him double.

[LAURIE *spots diners staring at* NICK]

Henry!

HENRY

Yes, Mr Blake.

LAURIE

Those diners over there are staring at Nick—get rid of them.

HENRY

Yes, sir. [HENRY *goes off to do as told*]

NICK

[*to* MIRANDA *about* SAINT JOHN] If we can crush Saint John, we're top of the heap.

LAURIE

We'll fuck him. We'll nail his balls to the wall. Let's buy BHP shares now, let's not wait. We'll send the price sky rocketing. Let's leave him millions of shares short on delivery day.

NICK

A dawn raid. [LAURIE *nods, pleased*]

MIRANDA

What's a dawn raid?

NICK

A swift, unexpected assault on the share market, with the help of friends.

[DAVID ASLOP, *editor of the* Herald, *looking confused and worried enters, he peers down at* nick *wondering if there has been an accident as* MIRANDA *pours* NICK *some more champagne*]

ASLOP

Is everything all right, Mr Blake?

LAURIE

Ah, Aslop. Yeh. No. That's why I wanted to see you.

ASLOP

It sounded urgent.

LAURIE

Urgent? [*Remembering*] Yes, I'll say it's fucking urgent. Tomorrow evening I am Australian of the Year. I'll be getting my prize from the PM himself.

ASLOP

And you deserve it, too.

LAURIE

Hold the cocksucking for a moment. You know that I am buying into some Romanian industries, [ASLOP *nods*] And yet you have an article in today's *Herald* criticising the Romanian government. How do you think that makes me look?

ASLOP

You're not suggesting interfering with editorial independence.

LAURIE

[*To whole of restaurant*] They always talk like child molesters.

[HENRY *comes over with a suit jacket and trousers and without a word being spoken holds them, while* LAURIE *takes off his cut suit and puts on the new one*—HENRY *standing in front of him, so the patrons cannot see him undressing,* LAURIE *continues on at* ASLOP *unconcerned*]

[*To* ASLOP] In tomorrow's paper I want to read a report about the good things in Romania.

ASLOP

The thing is, Mr Blake, we did keep certain things out of the newspaper. Aren't you a little concerned that Blake Industries sold Romania a centralised computer network?

LAURIE

Why should I be? They love it.

ASLOP

But it's being used by the secret police to keep tabs on every citizen.

LAURIE

What they want to do in their own country—

ASLOP

They can listen in on any phone call—

LAURIE

Listen Aslop—that computer system is Australian made. Blake Industries is creating exports for this fucking country. I want you to accentuate the positive. We're not all losers like you.

ASLOP

Are you telling me what to write?

LAURIE

[*clicking fingers, noticing champagne is finished*] Henry, more of the Dom! [*To* ASLOP] Yes, I am. I own it.

ASLOP

I resign. I resign on principle.

LAURIE

That means you've broken your contract. I'll get Johnson, your assistant, to edit tonight's paper.

ASLOP

He'll never do it.

LAURIE

Nick?

NICK

[*To* ASLOP] I spoke to him forty minutes ago. He's already putting the paper to bed now as we speak.

ASLOP

You are the most immoral man I've ever met.

[*He goes*]

LAURIE

Editors always sound like whores protesting they're virgins.

[A *male patron wearing only underpants and shoes crosses the restaurant on his way to the toilet, a bit tipsy. He yells out*]

PATRON

Good on ya, Blakey! You're what makes this country great!

LAURIE

[*yelling out*] Thanks for the clobber!

[HENRY *carrying the Dom, hurries up to* LAURIE]

HENRY

Sir, your wife is here.

LAURIE

What? I've told the staff not to double book us.

HENRY

A new member of staff made a mistake.

LAURIE

Who's she with?

HENRY

Some ladies.

LAURIE

Pissed?

HENRY

Under the weather.

LAURIE

Jesus, I had the brewery go into light beer just for her.

BRENDA

[*off*] You bastard!

LAURIE

Nick. Start pawing Miranda.

[NICK *hurries over to the table as best he can*]

[*To* HENRY] Stop her!

HENRY

Very good, sir.

[BRENDA *enters, furious*]

Mrs Blake—

BRENDA

Out of my way, poof.

LAURIE

Brenda, what are you doing here?

BRENDA

Late night meeting, eh?

[*Looking at* MIRANDA, *who is startled when* NICK *grabs her hand and kisses it repeatedly*]

LAURIE

I'm here with Nick. He's getting engaged.

BRENDA

Laurie, he's a eunuch.

LAURIE

He's been in Melbourne for the operation—they specialise in them down there.

BRENDA

[*storming over to the table. To* MIRANDA] I'll kill you if I see you with him again. Got it, bitch?

LAURIE

Brenda—

BRENDA

And I mean it.

LAURIE

You're becoming unstable. You cut my suits!

BRENDA

Because you're a two timing bastard.

LAURIE

Why don't you just get hot flushes like other women?

BRENDA

I found this. From Miranda. [*She waves a letter*] Written, I would say a couple of days ago, saying these past few weeks have been the happiest days of her life.

LAURIE

She's my art curator!

BRENDA

She also went on to say that, in her own words, 'It was the best sex' she ever had.

LAURIE

I could understand that.

BRENDA

Laurie! That's it, I want a divorce.

LAURIE

Have it! Have it! Look at you, you silly drunk. Look at the way you dress. Your screeching voice. Your make up—

BRENDA

[*shocked*] Laurie. You can't mean that. Think what we've been through together since we were teenagers. How could you say those things. I love you.

LAURIE

Divorce me. You're holding me back.

[BRENDA *bursts into tears*]

Bloody stop it.

[NICK *takes* LAURIE *out of earshot. distraught,* BRENDA *goes over to the table and downs* LAURIE's *champagne in a quick, savage gulp.*]

NICK

I wouldn't do that if I were you, Laurie.

LAURIE

Behind every successful man is an arsehole. She's giving me the pip. Searching through my pockets, whining, spending like there's no tomorrow.

NICK

That's the point, Laurie. She doesn't spend that much.

LAURIE

You live with her!

NICK

If she divorces you, she gets half of everything.

BRENDA

You are such a cruel man. What a bastard.

NICK

If she takes half, she's going to slow down our next move and you know how important that is.

LAURIE

[*knowing all too well*] Maybe we can make a deal with her.

BRENDA

I'm going to cut off your balls and take you for every penny you've got.

NICK

I think that kind of answers it, Laurie.

[LAURIE *reacts quickly. He takes her out of earshot of* MIRANDA]

LAURIE

I love you. I really do, my cutie pie. I'm taking Miranda out tonight to give her the boot. Then it'll be like the old days for us.

BRENDA

You mean that?

LAURIE

Yes, I do.

[*They kiss*]

BRENDA

I just went berserk—the letter—she's so beautiful.

LAURIE

Stop it—I love you.

BRENDA

I want a stud as proof of your love.

LAURIE

A stud?

BRENDA

A big one.

LAURIE

Aren't you a little old for one?

BRENDA

All my friends have got one.

LAURIE

Jeez, Brenda, how's it going to look—

BRENDA

I want one—

LAURIE

Christ, I suppose so, as long as you're discreet about it.

BRENDA

But the idea is to show it off.

LAURIE

I won't be cockholded like that. A man's got his pride.

NICK

I can whip down to the Cross and get one of those young guys—

BRENDA

Guys? [*Realising*] A diamond stud. I meant a diamond stud. Everyone I know's got one.

LAURIE

[*relieved*] All right. The biggest I can get you.

BRENDA

[*kissing him*] You're wonderful. [*Heading off, yelling out to friends*] Come on girls, let's hit a real restaurant. [*To* HENRY *as she exits*] You're not even a pimp, you're a pimple.

LAURIE

Ever get the feeling, Nick that men and women only have the language of money in common?

MIRANDA

What are you going to do about all of this?

LAURIE

I'm going to fire the guy who let Brenda in for a start—

then we'll finish the Dom.

[*He sits down*]

MIRANDA

Laurie—I mean Brenda—

LAURIE

She'll be fine—all she wanted was a stud. You're still the apple of my eye. [*Raising glass*] we're celebrating the Monet and the fall of Saints—[*The three clink glasses.* NICK *downing his champagne in one gulp*]

LAURIE

[*expansively to* NICK] It's a Dawn Raid, Nick!

NICK

And dawn has already started in England.

[LAURIE paws MIRANDA *with one hand and writes the order of events out on the table cloth for* NICK]

LAURIE

We'll be up all night. We'll move in on BHP through the English, then American, then Japanese markets as they open during the night, then jump on the Australian shares in the morning. A few parking arrangements wouldn't go astray.

MIRANDA

What are they?

LAURIE

It's where someone conceals his true ownership by having someone else buy and pretend to own the stocks.

MIRANDA

[*amused*] So what you're saying is that it's illegal?

LAURIE

It's only illegal if you don't get away with it.

MIRANDA

You're going to screw Saint John?

LAURIE

In the worst possible way.

[NICK *gets up and* LAURIE *whips the table cloth off the table and gives it to* NICK.]

MIRANDA

Can I keep it, Nick. After you've finished with it.

LAURIE

Why?

MIRANDA

The fate of an empire and who's going to be the richest man in Australia decided on a table cloth. [*Reminding* NICK *of his earlier words*] Like plugging into an electric socket.

LAURIE

Henry, fire the bastard who let Brenda in.

HENRY

Already done it, Mr Blake—he's heading out the front door now.

LAURIE

The back door, Henry. Get rid of incompetents out the back door. Oh, one thing, Henry, [LAURIE *gets up and walks* HENRY *out of* MIRANDA's *hearing*] See that good sort in the comer.

HENRY

Ms Crystal Lane.

LAURIE

Yeh, well that's where I want to park my truck. I want you to go over and tell her the Australian of the Year wants to see her later on. You know the address.

HENRY

[*nodding*] Very good, sir. [*He exits*]

LAURIE

[*looking at watch, to himself*] Give her a Laurie special and I'll be right for the whole night.

[LAURIE *returns to the table*]

[*To* MIRANDA] I'm going to have to shoot off, darling. A dawn raid needs a lot of preparation. [*Light kiss and then he and* NICK *head off*]

MIRANDA

[*disappointed*] Laurie ...!

[HENRY *goes over to the table*]

Share the champagne with me, Henry.

HENRY

[*sitting down*] What a night. I feel like a nun at a Buck's Party.

SCENE FOUR · THE KILLING FLOORS

LAURIE's *office. Day. A Monet in the background. A sense of urgency and excitement from* LAURIE *and* NICK. NICK *is speaking into two portable phones and is constantly looking at the three Rolexes on one arm.* LAURIE *is speaking into one and at the same time to* MIA *on the intercom. Dozens of phones ringing in the distance.*

NICK

I said buy! Buy! Buy! If you can't follow a simple instruction I'll fire you.

LAURIE

Buy every fucking thing you can.

NICK

Sam—use Nesbit Industries as a cover. Well, then use fucking Langdon Pipe Manufacturers as your parking arrangement.

LAURIE

Tell 'em is a fucking White Knight come to rescue BHP. [*Laughing*] The suckers. Yeh, it was us.

INTERCOM

Mr Blake—a journalist from the *Financial Review* wants to know if it was you who bought the London and New York shares—

LAURIE

[*amused, to* NICK] Fuck me, dead, if a journalist has figured it out—Saint John must know—[*To* MIA] Tell him to come and have a talk with me—

INTERCOM

Very good, sir.

LAURIE

[*to* NICK] I'll keep the fucker waiting for a few hours until we've cleaned up the Australian shares. How close are we?

NICK

Just about there—prices are going up—people are smelling a raid.

LAURIE

Like flies following a blood and bone truck. [*To caller on his phone*] Use Ward Consolidated to buy up those Melbourne shares. Fuck it! Now!

NICK

Grab them at 8.90. Go ten cents higher if you have to—

LAURIE

[*to* NICK] Close?

NICK

Apparently during the making of porno movies the crew have to stand around waiting for the guy to get an erection. They call it 'waiting for wood'... we're close to getting wood. Just waiting on Thommo to talk Dekel into selling.

LAURIE

[*putting down his phone*] Great! The perfect dawn raid. No sleep in over twenty-four hours and I feel great.

NICK

No rest for the wicked, Laurie.

[*Wearing sunglasses,* SAINT JOHN *enters*]

INTERCOM

Mr Blake! Mr Blake! Mr Saint John pushed his way into your office.

LAURIE

That's OK, Mia. That's fine. [*Smiling*] Ah, Baz, how's tricks?

ST JOHN

[*Attempting to be cheery*] Just fine.

LAURIE

Bit of trouble in the market today, Baz?

ST JOHN

How did you hear?

LAURIE

A journo rang me.

ST JOHN

Nothing I can't handle.

[ST JOHN *notices* NICK *whispering frantically into his two portable phones, then turns back to* LAURIE]

There has been a huge push on BHP from a few areas. Can't put my finger on it on who or why.

LAURIE

[*enjoying this*] Don't understand, Baz.

ST JOHN

You know how I said I'd deliver three hundred million BHP shares to match yours? Well, immediately after speaking to you—ah ... [ST JOHN *notices* NICK *smirking and pauses and then looks back at* LAURIE *who is also smirking.*]

LAURIE

You gambled that the share price would fall and buy your shares back at a lower price and make a tidy profit at my expense. The share prices have actually risen leaving you—I'd say, half a billion dollars short.

ST JOHN

[*Surprised*] Yes. I mean—

NICK

[*sudden, triumphant yell*] Yo, Laurie! We've got wood! We've got wood!

LAURIE

[LAURIE *claps his hands with joy*] You're done like a dinner, Baz. Financially stretched in England, the States and now here.

ST JOHN

[*Noticing* NICK's *three Rolexes, realising*] You did it! [*pointing to them*] London time. New York time. Australia.

LAURIE

Hey, not that many shares. That would be illegal. I'd have to announce a BHP takeover.

ST JOHN

You've got parking arrangements. Why, what was the point? We were going to be partners.

LAURIE

People ask me why I do something. I answer, 'Why should I not do it?'

NICK

Laurie's into Zen.

LAURIE

Yeh, why do I do things, Baz?

[*He grabs knife and slashes the Monet much to* SAINT JOHN *and* NICK's *horror*]

Like that. Because I like to play for keeps. You're terminated, Baz. You'll never get out of this financial black hole. [*Advancing, cold and relentless. He whips* SAINT JOHN's *sunglasses off him*] Let's see the whites of your eyes. Without your sunnies, Baz, your eyes are a dead give away. I have seen that look, many, many times. It's the look of fear. You see it in an animal's eyes when it's about to be slaughtered. They enter the chute, a bit nervous. But confident, but as they advance down the chute into the killing rooms, they smell blood. They look around and see men with these things in their hand. And although they are not terrified yet, they are afraid. Their eyes grow large and twitch. Hands grab them, sure, certain hands. Hands that have done this a thousand times. The animals are locked into a position they struggle against but cannot escape from. You place the stun gun behind the back of their ear and the feeling of the metal, the sense of being trapped—at that split second, they know. They are going to die. Before the whack, there is such a look of terror and fear in their eyes that you never forget it. You're looking into the soul of an animal and seeing the greatest terror a man can see in another beast. That look is there, in your eyes, Baz.

[ST JOHN *is rattled*]

ST JOHN

I'll get back at you.

LAURIE

You can't. I've killed you. You're a ghost.

[ST JOHN *goes. Pause*]

NICK

[*impressed*] King of the Castle, Laurie.

[LAURIE *nods, satisfied*]

LAURIE

Lost his balls. We'll courier over some bullock's balls to him.

[*Both laugh,* NICK *looks at the slashed Monet.*]

NICK

Expensive way to make a point, though.

LAURIE

Eh? No. It's a reproduction. The real one's in the bank vault. [*Looking at watch*] Better put the boots on. Tonight's the big night. The highest point in my career. I've got a new suit. Looks snazzy. The PM will be there. The Treasurer—did he accept?

NICK

Yes.

LAURIE

NO one cares about the PM, but you always return the Treasurer's calls.

NICK

You think they're going to be pissed off about Romania?

LAURIE

Crikey dick—everyone goes on in Australia about human rights in South Africa, but the government secretly deals with them. Romania! I met Ceausescu and his wife. Christ, they're not monsters. You see husbands and wives like them down at the RSL every night. [*Looking at watch*] Jesus, I'm Australian of the Year in a couple of hours—where's that suit? Up thirty odd hours and I feel as good as new. I want you to send a fax to Miranda, tell her it was fun but things have changed. Give her the deed of the apartment.

NICK

What about the Blake's Art Gallery?

LAURIE

She can continue to run it but its not my priority now. Crystal's a gym instructor. I'm going to start gym franchises in the States for her.

NICK

What if Miranda kicks up a fuss?

LAURIE

Give her the Streeton.

[*He goes off to the bathroom of his suite.* NICK *looks around to make sure* LAURIE *doesn't see him and puts some coke on the table, takes out his Amex card and divides it up into some hefty lines*]

LAURIE

[*off*] If Brenda cuts up my new suits I'm going to have her bumped off. Isn't this a great land! Where else could a truckie like me become Australian of the Year. The wealthiest man in Australia. Pictures of me everywhere.

Women journos leave wet patches on chairs after interviewing me.

[NICK *is not listening as he concentrates on snorting the coke.*]

That Crystal's a bit of a goer. Do you want to marry my daughter?

[NICK *sneezes at the thought, sending his coke everywhere*]

NICK

[*Cry of alarm*] Oh, no!

LAURIE

You don't?

NICK

[*Scraping coke together*] She's only fourteen.

LAURIE

Keep it in the family.

NICK

I'm not a full man, Laurie.

LAURIE

[*entering, putting on suit jacket*] Well, that's OK, she's not a woman yet. [*Noticing the coke*] What's that?

NICK

Talcum powder—my doctor said I had to take it internally.

LAURIE

You're not buckling under pressure, Nick?

NICK

Me? I eat stress for breakfast!

LAURIE

Baby powder's a constant market. I can buy Johnson's and Johnson's for you, if you like?

NICK

No, it's fine, Laurie.

LAURIE

Great—because I'd hate you to buckle under on my night of all nights. Don't be late. [*Before going, turning back triumphantly to* NICK] I'm the Jesus Christ of entrepreneurs—I smash temples!

[LAURIE *exits*]

NICK

[*laughing to himself*] Baby powder! [*To audience*] There you are. Dressed to kill. Wetting your pants at the thought of being in his presence. I can't believe there is so much money in this audience. How much power. Never have so few owed so much, to so many. [*He laughs*]

SCENE FIVE · EXPAND OR DIE

Smoke and fog swirl across the stage. In the background is a huge sign 'Blake Industries'. LAURIE *comes out with a microphone, looking tremendously happy. Wild applause for him.*

LAURIE

[*fake modesty*] Enough. Enough. Thank you. No, no, that's enough.

[*Pause*]

This is a special moment for me. To be here, in front of you. In front of the whole of Australia really. And most importantly, my staff. Blake Industries is now the largest employer in the whole of Australia. And yet, all this is not due to me.

[BRENDA *enters in another expensive fashion disaster but looking very happy.*]

It's due to you, Australia, but also due to my wife—Brenda. [*They kiss*]

BRENDA

If there were more people like my husband, Australia would be the wealthiest country in the whole world.

[*Lights come up on either side of the stage. On one side,* NICK *is sniffing a few more lines of coke. He has a maniacal smile. On the other side is* MIRANDA, *drinking whiskey, brooding about events*]

LAURIE

We can be wealthy. The whole lot of us. Because private enterprise works! Without interference from the government the economy is working. Almost at full steam. What do I mean by 'almost'? Well, the Labor Government has been absolutely fantastic in ridding themselves of the old victim ideology. But they still have a way to go. Yes, you know what I mean: someone's poor therefore it's our fault. Our fault! It's bloody their fault. They don't work—they bludge—off you and me. [*A beat*] I've heard the rumours, so has Brenda ... people saying Laurie Blake should go into politics and get this country full steam ahead. Well, to be honest, I have heard the bushfire of my name burning through the grassroots out there. I've also been approached by a political party and I am thinking about it. As Prime Minister I would do nothing about the economy, except get rid of the rules and regulations and I'd let private enterprise run the economy. On my television station from tonight, will be an advertisement, celebrating my workers and my philosophy, but I'll give you a taste of the song that goes with it. Why, will I inflict my voice on you? Because I believe every single word. I wrote them! [*Cheers*] [*Music starts up and* LAURIE *sings*]

LAURIE

You can tread the water
of the ocean of life
and all you do is drown
You can jump up and down
[but] you stay in the same place
and you won't win the race.

You can sharpen a knife
Pick your teeth free of meat
but if you don't take a life
then you'll end in defeat

Let your friends get ahead
then you need your head read.

SEIZE THE DAY
OR LET IT GO AWAY
KEEP ON THE GO
DON'T ASK WHY
ALL YOU NEED TO KNOW
IS EXPAND OR DIE!

[LAURIE *bows, acknowledging applause.* MIRANDA *holds sleeping pills in one hand and drinks from a whiskey glass held in the other.* NICK *finishes a line of coke and looks out at the audience*]

MIRANDA

[*to herself, very matter of factly*] There is the painting by Jacques Louis David—Socrates—before his students and followers—about to drink a bowl of hemlock. He is calm and straightforward about it all ...

NICK

[*to audience, beaming like a maniac*] Dressed to kill. Thinking you're the ants pants. I can't believe there is so much money in this audience. How much power. Never have so few owed so much, to so many. I eat stress!

[MIRANDA *downs the pills*]

LAURIE

Thank you. Thank you. Prime Minister. Treasurer. The world awaits us. Expand or die!

ACT THREE

SCENE ONE · THIS IS THE LIFE

A ballroom in Monte Carlo. A fancy dress ball in progress. Distant orchestra. Palms. Brilliant, wealthy, upper class people. BRENDA, *dressed as Marilyn Monroe, sips champagne watching it all wide-eyed as royalty and famous names dance by. She curtsies as some* VIP *goes past.* LAURIE, *dressed as Ned Kelly, enters. He approaches* BRENDA *and says something,* BRENDA *cannot understand him because he is wearing the helmet.*

BRENDA

Take it off, I can't hear you.

LAURIE

[*taking it off*] Where's Helen?

BRENDA

Somewhere in there dancing with one of the Monaco princes.

LAURIE

Why's she dancing with him, he's a poof.

BRENDA

Laurie, don't be like that. Oh, look Princess Stephanie.

[BRENDA *curtsies,* LAURIE *is uninterested in royalty and looks at businessmen in the crowds.*]

LAURIE

I bought his helicopter business.

BRENDA

Never did I think we'd be at such a party in Monte Carlo.

LAURIE

[*motioning to someone else*] I took over his clothing factories.

BRENDA

Ever since I saw that film with Grace Kelly and Cary Grant.

LAURIE

I bought his munitions empire. Plus his airship.

BRENDA

There's so many royalty I don't know whether to curtesy or lay flat on my back.

LAURIE

Whatever comes naturally, Brenda.

BRENDA

Aren't you excited, Laurie?

LAURIE

Yeh, Freddie Arrow's here.

BRENDA

Is he some sort of royalty.

LAURIE

Unlike royalty he's got money. The poms are always so up themselves, aren't they? Now I own most of the English newspapers and TV stations, they're not so smug. Thatcher wants me to support her in her Poll Tax fight. I'll keep her hanging for while.

[HELEN *comes over, dressed like a woman out of Watteau*]

BRENDA

You look lovely, darling.

HELEN

Thanks mum.

LAURIE

How did the tennis practice go today?

HELEN

OK.

LAURIE

The best money can buy. Your coach won five grand slams.

BRENDA

She's got a long way to go, Laurie.

LAURIE

Nonsense, she's going to be better than Goolagong. [*Spotting* FREDDIE ARROW *crossing room*] There's Arrow.

[ARROW *is dressed as a pirate with a stuffed parrot on his shoulder*]

[*To* HELEN] Listen, darling—go and have a bit of a dance with Freddie Arrow.

HELEN

Why?

LAURIE

See what he thinks of me. I'm going to take him over.

BRENDA

Laurie—you can't use your own daughter as a gigolo.

LAURIE

Christ, I'm not going to dance with him. [*Kissing* HELEN *on cheek*] One for your dad.

[HELEN *goes over to Arrow and introduces herself. He is a bit surprised at her forwardness—they dance*]

BRENDA

Laurie!

LAURIE

Arrow owns half of Europe, he's got some of the biggest industries in Europe and he owns parts of the Monopoly board I want.

BRENDA

Now, I remember him—doesn't he have a terrible reputation with the ladies, even though he's married?

LAURIE

He can get a divorce.

BRENDA

What are you talking about?

LAURIE

He could marry Helen.

BRENDA

Laurie, he's in his middle sixties

LAURIE

So, he wouldn't last long. Cardiac arrest in the arms of our daughter.

BRENDA

If we weren't in a public place I'd throttle you. I'm going to put on a bit more lippy. [*She exits*]

[LAURIE *smiles to himself as she watches* ARROW *and* HELEN *dancing*]

LAURIE

[*to himself*] Dance, Arrow, dance. I'll soon own all of the Monopoly board and you. [*Putting on his helmet*] Time to rob a few banks.

[NICK *enters, coked to the eyeballs, dressed as a punk, with pink mohawk hair. He walks quickly on his crutches.*]

NICK

[*To himself*] Everyone's dancing so slowly. My heart's pounding, racing like a rabbit. Breathe in. Breathe out. Ah, that's better. Things are looking good. Maybe a couple more lines to be fully in tune. Harmonic chemical alignment. [*Starts to go*]

[LAURIE *walks past, dressed as a Ned Kelly. He doesn't recognise* NICK, NICK *is startled to see Ned Kelly*]

Fuck me dead!

LAURIE

[*startled*] Nick. Didn't recognise you.

NICK

Who are you? Get out of my mind! [*Yelling*] Bouncer! Get me a bouncer!

LAURIE

[*taking off helmet*] It's me—Laurie.

NICK

Christ—I thought I was hallucinating for a moment.

LAURIE

They'll throw you out dressed like that.

NICK

What do you mean, I won first prize.

LAURIE

I'm as famous as Ned Kelly, so I thought I'd come as him.

NICK

Saw Helen with that cocksucker, Arrow.

LAURIE

I want you to ring through to London. Buy into five per cent of Arrow.

NICK

We haven't got the money—we're over extended at the moment.

LAURIE

Fuck the money, buy into him! Use a shelf company, so he doesn't know it's us.

NICK

Way to go, Laurie!

LAURIE

Get London to organise our trip to Romania. We'll tie up the ore deal with Ceausescu—that should keep the banks happy.

NICK

Don't you ever rest, Laurie.

LAURIE

[*motioning to* ARROW *dancing with* HELEN] Look at him. He's resting, while I'm screwing him.

NICK

[*to his own feet*] Feets, do your stuff.

LAURIE

You OK?

NICK

On top of the world. On top of the world, Laurie. I was thinking of giving that cunt Ceausescu a run for his money. We'll tell the short arse to come across with another billion. He's got his people down to two hours worth of electricity a night, he can force them to make do with one hour a night. Then he could give us the extra billion. A million lightbulbs of ideas are lighting up my head, Laurie.

LAURIE

[*making joke*] But who's going to pay your electricity bill? [*Motioning to hair*] This is not permanent, Nick?

NICK

Been thinking about making the wig real. That'd scare the fuck out of some Boards of Management.

LAURIE

You think you need a rest, Nick?

NICK

I'm in balance right now, Laurie.

LAURIE

You think Thatcher is a good root? I mean, do you often

wonder things like that, Nick? Does Denis come home after a round of golf and a few G and Ts and give her a bit of the crab stick doggie style?

NICK

Don't think about that sort of thing much, Laurie.

LAURIE

Yeh, success makes me reflective. Tell London to get me an appointment with Maggie tomorrow arvo. I'll support her on the Poll Tax if she gives me TV AM. [*A beat*] I think I'll go eavesdrop on Freddie and Helen.

[LAURIE *heads over to woman dressed as Cleopatra and wearing a mask.*]

NICK

If you see that fucker Prince Rainier tell him I want to see him. [*Spotting passing waiter*] Hey, Frog, where's the telephone? Hey, escargot, ou est le telephone? [*The waiter passes not acknowledging* NICK. *To himself*] Fuckin' snail ... feeling good ... wired for sound. [NICK *exits*]

[LAURIE *has approached the woman and they start to dance.*]

WOMAN

You dance well.

[LAURIE is *trying to move her towards* HELEN *and* FREDDIE.]

LAURIE

Yeh, yeh.

WOMAN

I knew that you would know how to dance, Laurie.

LAURIE

[*pleasantly surprised*] You've heard of me?

WOMAN

I know you, Laurie.

LAURIE

Me?

WOMAN

You gave me a going over ...

LAURIE

Enjoy it?

WOMAN

As I think about it more and more ... no.

LAURIE

I don't remember you.

WOMAN

We once spent an afternoon together.

LAURIE

Sorry, love, I—

[*The woman takes off mask: it is* TERRY BURCHETT *in drag.*]

Christ ... Terry.

WOMAN

Burchett.

[LAURIE *jumps away as if bitten.*]

LAURIE

What in hell are you doing here?

WOMAN

Every year the Rainiers invite me to their fancy dress ball …

LAURIE

Are the rest round-the-corner merchants like you?

WOMAN

I'm getting a bit tired of it, I admit. I'm thinking of going into business.

LAURIE

Yeh, pigs will fly.

WOMAN

You do, Laurie.

LAURIE

I need a drink. [*He exits,* TERRY *puts his mask back on and exits the other way laughing as* FREDDIE *and* HELEN *dance downstage.*]

FREDDIE

Something out of a Watteau painting.

HELEN

Yes. You guessed.

FREDDIE

You look as lovely as one of Watteau's beautiful women.

HELEN

Thank you.

FREDDIE

Your accent—I detect Australian gum trees.

HELEN

Yes. I'm from Sydney.

FREDDIE

Lovely city. Been there a few times.

HELEN

Do you live in Monte Carlo?

FREDDIE

Sometimes. London mostly. And you?

HELEN

Australia. England. Dad's based in England a bit more. He's Laurie Blake.

[FREDDIE *tries to hide his distaste*]

FREDDIE

Oh, yes, he moored his yacht next to mine this morning, yelling out, 'Mine's bigger than yours'. I thought he was some yankee who was going to moon me or something. First appearances are deceptive. To have a lovely daughter like you, he must have something special.

[BRENDA *enters,* LAURIE *has been watching* FREDDIE *and* HELEN]

LAURIE

Come on, darl—let's dance.

BRENDA

[*pleased*] Oh, Laurie, we haven't danced in ages.

LAURIE

Yeh, well, you're the only real woman here.

[*He quickly dances her towards* FREDDIE *and* HELEN]

[*to* HELEN] How's it going, darling?

HELEN

Mum. Dad. I'd like you to meet Freddie Arrow.

BRENDA

Hello.

LAURIE

G'day.

FREDDIE

Hello.

LAURIE

Like my yacht? [*Proudly*] The biggest here.

FREDDIE

Oh, really …?

LAURIE

Yeh, and it's got a special keel.

[*The couples dance side by side*]

FREDDIE

You have a wild colonial boy's chirpiness, Mr Blake.

LAURIE

My financial wizard, Nick Albert.

NICK

The convicts strike back. You thought you could dump

us in Australia, but we're back. We've come to take everything you've got, screw your wives and steal your daughters.

FREDDIE

You never know, Laurie, you may return to your convict status sooner than you think.

NICK

We've had to bring in Australians to run our organisations in England.

FREDDIE

Is this like an Australian sport—pommy bashing?

LAURIE

Christ, I even bought a whole village. A village! No Australian village would sell itself like a bunch of smurfs. The pommies are the Nigerians of the West.

BRENDA

Laurie!

HELEN

Dad!

[*But* LAURIE *is enjoying this*]

FREDDIE

You know nothing about business ethics.

LAURIE

It's a contradiction in terms. I've got you, Freddie. By the balls—I've just got five per cent of them.

FREDDIE

What do you mean?

NICK

Nine per cent!

LAURIE

Nine?

NICK

London was so pleased with the idea of the Romanian deal—we got an extra billion. So I said lets fuck Arrow well and truly.

LAURIE

Great! Great! [*Back to* FREDDIE] We're going to take you over, Freddie. Go and play with your little boat.

FREDDIE

[*well mannered, to* BRENDA] Excuse me, Mrs Blake. [*To* HELEN] Thank you for the dance, Miss Blake.

[*furious,* FREDDIE *goes,* LAURIE *smiles triumphantly*]

We'll blow torch him, Nick.

BRENDA

[*to* LAURIE] Was that really necessary?

LAURIE

Yeh—it made coming to the party worthwhile. Let's go and buy a castle. [*Off they go*]

BRENDA

[*pleased*] One that has those servants that dress like ushers at the old Dendy?

LAURIE

Whatever.

[HELEN *and* NICK *are left alone*]

HELEN

He's only happy making deals.

NICK

[*a cold shiver of fear runs up his spine*] Jesus—get a load of those lizards.

HELEN

Lizards?

NICK

Big as fucking horses.

HELEN

Dad's ruined another night. I'm going to get drunk. [*She goes*]

NICK

[to *himself*] Pretend the lizards aren't there. Tell Rainier where to get off. Come on, Nick—show the cunt where to get off. [*Yelling out, fist in the air*] Anarchy in the UK! [*He exits in search of Rainier.*]

SCENE TWO · WAITING FOR THE BARBARIANS

The fields in the English countryside, LAURIE, *dressed in an English hunting outfit enters with shotgun. In the distance we hear dozens of yelling voices. Dogs. Beaters. He looks for his quarry and suddenly sees a partridge fly up. He shoots. But misses.*

LAURIE

Shit!

[A *local villager, the head beater, enters dressed in raincoat and battered hat.*]

Bloody quick buggers, Reggie.

REGGIE

[*Somerset accent*] That they are, Mr Blake.

LAURIE

You sure they know what they're doing?

REGGIE

For five hundred years this village has had the best beaters in England, sir.

LAURIE

Maybe you've grown stale.

REGGIE

There was no complaints from Sir Andrew, Mr Blake.

LAURIE

He was eighty when he sold your village. Probably hadn't fired a gun in years.

REGGIE

I would like to have a word with you, sir about—[*Sounds of fox hunt: hounds. Horns. 'Tally-ho'*]

LAURIE

Hey, what are those fox hunters doing on my land?

REGGIE

They're allowed through these fields over here: 'The Corridor of the Hunt'.

LAURIE

Who gave them that right?

REGGIE

The Normans, sir.

LAURIE

I'll bloody sue them. [*Spotting bird*] There's a partridge. [*He swings around and shoots,* REGGIE *ducks and yells out a warning.*]

REGGIE

Riders!

[LAURIE *rushes off in the opposite direction in search of partridges*]

Sir, are you all right?

[*Sound of gun shots from* LAURIE, *limping* FREDDIE ARROW *dressed in a coveted pink hunting jacket enters.*]

FREDDIE

Some fool almost shot my horse. It tripped. [*Waving to others, calling out*] I'm all right! After the fox! After the fox!

[LAURIE *enters*]

LAURIE

Bloody quick buggers those partridges. [*Noticing* ARROW. *Beaming*] Well, well, Freddie Arrow, have a bit of a spill, did we?

FREDDIE

[*stunned*] Blake ...

LAURIE

This is my village. Those are my villagers beating for me. Once I sue the Normans you won't be able to use my fields for your hunts.

[ARROW *grimaces in pain and feels his leg.*]

Soon, you'll be hurting all over, Freddie. I've bought another six percent of you. Here, in these English fields—surrender.

FREDDIE

We fought for Cromwell—we don't surrender.

LAURIE

[*Spotting bird*] There's one! [*He rushes off*]

FREDDIE

[*to* REGGIE] What is happening to England? Australians are everywhere. Can't watch television without that fat-know-it-all Clive James pontificating. Then there's that loopy harridan Germaine Greer: she's ruined relations between the sexes for the past twenty years. Every time I turn on a talk show there's that bloody Australian drag queen. Murdoch's turning *The Times* into *MacTimes.* Packer winning at polo. That Gyngell fellow who runs TV AM, examining his stools like some Bavarian sausage connoisseur. Now I know how the Ancient Romans felt when the barbarians were at the gates of Rome.

REGGIE

That is right, sir. That is right.

[BARRY SAINT JOHN *enters, wearing sunglasses and an ordinary fox hunting outfit*]

ST JOHN

You all right, Freddie?

FREDDIE

Fine, Barry. Slight twinge of the knee. My horse, it doesn't look the best.

LAURIE

[*entering*] Well, well, well ... If it isn't Baz St. John.

ST JOHN

[*Not enjoying this*] Laurie ...

LAURIE

Still the sunnies, even in England's weak light.

FREDDIE

Barry and I went to the same school.

LAURIE

[*to* ARROW] I snipped off Baz's balls, but he's got enough dough, obviously. [*To* SAINT JOHN] This is my village. They're all beating for me.

REGGIE

That's what I want to talk to you about, guv'nor.

LAURIE

[*To* ARROW *and* SAINT JOHN] Don't you just love the way they talk.

REGGIE

Since you bought our village the rates have sky rocketed.

LAURIE

Because you cost so much to buy!

REGGIE

We're a poor village, sir. We can't afford it.

LAURIE

Fuck me dead! A couple of centuries ago, the Lord of the Manor would have cut off your head for just looking at him and raped your wife. Just work harder. Look at alt those beaters slacking off. Go tell them to get off their arses.

[REGGIE *goes,* SAINT JOHN *and* ARROW *are appalled at* LAURIE's *behaviour*]

FREDDIE

My horse. It's in a bad way. Can I borrow your gun and put it out of its misery.

[LAURIE *points gun at* ARROW]

LAURIE

Why don't I put you out of your misery, Freddie?

[FREDDIE *steps back, worried that* LAURIE *will*]

Too easy. I'll leave the London Stock Exchange to do it. I'll tell you what, Freddie. I'll bump off your horse and in return you come Down Under to my daughter's wedding.

Deal? [LAURIE *does not wait for an answer. He spots a horse off*] The one with the limp?

[FREDDIE *nods,* LAURIE *goes off*]

FREDDIE

His takeover bid has upped the share price so much, the shareholders are certain to sell. [*On to another tack, remembering, angry*] Waving to me from his yacht in Monto Carlo like some peasant who won the pools. I should have concentrated more.

ST JOHN

Do you want to get him?

FREDDIE

Maybe I'm too old. Maybe I should just sell it to him.

[*Gunshot*]

Christ—he's missed! [*A beat*] I'd love to get him, Barry. Love to.

ST JOHN

You can. I've wanted to get back at him for years. I've collected a lot of information on him. He's more financially overextended than anyone knows. His debt to ratio figures are appalling. So highly geared that his business empire is like a stack of cards.

FREDDIE

That would explain his constant leveraged buy outs.

ST JOHN

Warehousing. Insider trading. He's into it all. The thing that's keeping him going is that even the banks don't know how highly geared he is. He's paid too much for every business he's bought recently. Then there's the junk bonds .... All it needs is someone to bring all these things to light and the banks will have nothing to do with him. He wouldn't have the assets to pay back even the interest.

[*Gunshot,* FREDDIE *grimaces*]

FREDDIE

At least he's put it out of its pain. If I could prove all that, then I'd keep him from the door of Arrow industries.

ST JOHN

And finish him completely.

LAURIE

[*entering*] It moves fast for a horse with a broken leg. I know you poms wouldn't have the stomach to do it. Well, see ya, have a good walk back to the village. And remember, business means never having to say you're sorry! [*To himself*] Now for those fucking birds. [*He heads off in the other direction*]

[FREDDIE ARROW *is livid at how he has been treated.*]

FREDDIE

That man ... I will destroy him, Barry. What you destroy is his aura. His image. You dirty his name. Because he depends on the fame of his name, then you besmirch that name. So that in the end the name Blake will be what you say when you spit.

SCENE THREE · HUMANS ARE ONLY MEAT

NICK, *unshaven and untidy in his darkened office staring at the lights of Sydney in between sniffing some lines of coke. The radio is on.*

RADIO

Mr Freddie Arrow continued his attack on Mr Laurie Blake today in what seems a deliberate campaign to undermine investor and bank confidence in his empire. Mr Arrow accused the Blake empire of being massively in debt and having no real assets to take over his company. In fact, said Mr Arrow, Mr Blake's empire is a house of cards and is nothing more than pyramid selling. In reply Mr Blake said that Mr Arrow was running scared and that the Egyptians built pyramids and they've lasted two thousand years—as his empire will. Financial journalists—

NICK

[to *radio, sneering*] Financial journalists!

[NICK *turns off radio with remote control*]

[*To himself*] How many financial journalists does it take to change a light bulb—None!—They don't even know what a light bulb is. [*Looking at lights of Sydney*] Hey, you, down there! You want to turn against us? Try, just try—you won't succeed Freddie, Barry, because I know how the world runs. I've learnt what makes it go. [*To audience*] The world is a sewer and only the rats know it. And rats are just furry pieces of meat. That's all we humans are: meat. We are born a crying piece of bloody meat. Some of us are intelligent pieces of meat. Others, stupid. The stupid ones—like you—end up hanging in a butcher's shop. The intelligent ones? They are the ones that know that love is another word for fucking, money is to survive, and that there is no afterlife; only the rotting of your carcass. So you live for now. Given that's all you are, pieces of meat, what you've got to decide in this life is whether you are going to end up hanging from a hook in a butcher's shop. Or are you going to hook someone else up.

SCENE FOUR · FOR RICHER, FOR POORER

LAURIE's *house. Night. A patio. Fairy lights. One waiter carrying drinks tray enters from one side of stage while* HENRY, *the other waiter, enters from the other. They drink the champagne dregs. The wedding reception is inside with music, dancing and laughter. We hear the prime minister.*

PM

[*on microphone as waiters talk*] Laurie Blake is one of the great Australians. Without him Australia would be a very different country. He made us proud to be Australian. It was because of him that the whole world stood up and took notice of us as we launched ourselves like warriors onto Europe and America ....

WAITER

Biggest wedding ever.

HENRY

I might slip some ground glass to Blake's poodles, they're weeing on all the flower arrangements.

[*They stop and listen to a little of the speech*]

WAITER

I've been serving the guys from Milson's Industries—

HENRY

Heard anything?

WAITER

They look like taking over IXL.

HENRY

Good, I have a few shares, might sell them tomorrow and make a bit. What about Blake?

WAITER

I don't know ... a few rumours going around that Arrow's campaign is making investors uneasy—I've got a few Blake shares ... I might sell.

HENRY

He's as safe as houses. Long term investment for my retirement. Christ, I wish the Prime Minister would shut up!

PM

Laurie Blake's financial wizardry transformed Australia. Jeez, if he were a woman I'd give him a big kiss of thanks, but, instead I'll have to kiss his daughter [*Laughter*] So a big thank you to a great Australian and his lovely daughter.

[*Applause*]

WAITER

Back into the fray.

HENRY

Oh, god, here comes Fatal Unattraction.

BRENDA

[*entering*] Moonlighting from Pandora's, Henry?

HENRY

Mr Blake wanted someone experienced—

BRENDA

Still hooning for him—

HENRY

I resent—

BRENDA

Get in there—keep an eye on the Romanian ambassador—he's nicking the cutlery.

HENRY

Which one is he?

BRENDA

You'll recognise him—he's part of the universal Brotherhood too.

[*As the waiters exit, she whips a glass of champagne from one of the trays. Downs half of it in one gulp, then she gasps in surprise, a figure suddenly appears out of the darkness. It is* NICK, *a mobile phone hanging from a strap around his neck He is wearing a grubby, food stained suit and is unshaven and dirty*]

You startled me, Nick.

NICK

Am I late?

BRENDA

This is a wedding reception, Nick. You look terrible. My god, how long is it since you had a bath?

NICK

Haven't had time, Brenda. Could you go and get Laurie for me?

BRENDA

Aren't you going to come in?

NICK

Hate crowds.

BRENDA

Good, because you pong. [*She exits*]

[NICK's *mobile phone rings. He flops to the ground and answers it*]

Yeh, it's me. Who did you think it was? The messiah? Listen, shit head, just give me the info on Tokyo. [*listening*] Haven't you got contacts with the Yakuza? Bump off the managers. Wimp! [*he stops the call*]

LAURIE

[*enters, peering into darkness*] Nick?

NICK

Over here.

LAURIE

How's it going ... is there a run? [*Startled by* NICK*'s appearance*] You look a mess.

NICK

What are you, the style mafia or something?

LAURIE

Sorry, Nick—

NICK

We could get the mafia to bump off Freddie Arrow. [*Chuckling to himself*] Hey, we could get the IRA—tell them Arrow's funding the Protestants.

LAURIE

Nick, we can't kill anyone.

NICK

You're going soft, Laurie.

LAURIE

The Prime Minister's brown nosing me. But he's asking me about New York.

NICK

Tell him it was an aberration.

LAURIE

Half our American stock was wiped off.

NICK

It's Tokyo that we have to worry about. [*He looks at the four watches he now has attached to one wrist*] The stock exchange is opening in a few minutes. If there's a run on our stock there—then Australia will quickly follow suit, you know what brown noses Australians are, then tomorrow the English will finish us—Arrow will be their hero. [*Tapping phone*] I've got my finger on the pulse.

LAURIE

There's a lot of balls being juggled at the moment, Nick—don't forget that two of them are mine. I'll go and stroke the PM a little more.

[LAURIE *goes inside. A waiter passes*]

NICK

Hey, Henry.

HENRY

[*startled*] Yes, Mr Albert—

NICK

[*whispering*] Got any coke?

HENRY

Are you sure you don't want a bath?

NICK

Course, I fucking don't—Now get me some coke.

[HENRY *goes.* NICK *is jittery*]

[*To himself*] The IRA would love to bump Arrow off. Laurie's turning soft.

[HELEN *comes out, lost in thought, half pleased, half brooding. She is still wearing her wedding dress.*]

Congratulations, Helen.

HELEN

Nick!

NICK

Sorry, I couldn't see you get hitched but I was busy.

HELEN

You're always busy.

NICK

Where the hubby?

HELEN

Wayne's in there. Working the room. Should never have married an economist.

NICK

Yeh, you must have some deep seated resentment against Laurie to go and to that. They'll miss you if you stay out here.

HELEN

No, they're not my friends. They're dad's business

friends. All the politicians, bankers, journos—they want to see him. More popular than the Prime Minister someone said to me tonight.

NICK

Tide's turning.

HELEN

What are you talking about?

NICK

Lips are sealed.

HELEN

Still, it was a grand wedding. The biggest. I'll always remember that. Like Cinderella. You should have married. There are other things besides work.

NICK

Ever read that William Faulkner novel, the one about the corn cob and the girl?

HELEN

What are you on?

NICK

Did the Treasurer turn up?

HELEN

No.

NICK

[to *himself*] Oh, Jesus ... where's that fuckin' waiter?

NICK

Where's that fuckin' waiter! [*Phone rings. Irritated, answering* it] Yes!

[*He listens, more concerned by the minute,* LAURIE *comes out*]

HELEN

Nick's on drugs, dad.

LAURIE

Nonsense, he's overworked. Go inside. Mingle. It's your wedding.

HELEN

It's yours. [*He looks surprised*] Doesn't matter, I'll do as you say.

LAURIE

That a girl. [LAURIE *goes over to* NICK] How's it going?

NICK

[*putting hand over mouthpiece*] There's a run on our shares in Tokyo. Arrow again. [LAURIE *shakes his head*]

LAURIE

All that information about me that Arrow keeps passing on to the press.

NICK

But it's true, Laurie. The banks are threatening to jump on us.

[SIMON *wanders out with drink in his hand looking very pleased with himself.*]

NICK

[*whispering*] Get that prick Simon to give us a couple of billion. We can restore confidence in our shares before the Australian market opens in the morning and we can stop the run on them in England. [*To phone caller*] Tell the slant eyes, they'll pay for this. [*Ferociously switches off phone*]

LAURIE

Simon ... enjoying yourself?

SIMON

[*excitedly*] Shook hands with the Prime Minister, pity the Treasurer couldn't make it.

LAURIE

You're looking great. [*Admiring clothes*] Now, see, if it wasn't for me, you would never have known your Armani from your Woolies, never have shaken hands with the PM.

SIMON

Well—

LAURIE

Be honest. You're top in your bank, now. You've made them a small fortune. A big one actually.

SIMON

We'd make more if you and a few others starting paying your interest loans on time.

LAURIE

I've always eventually paid up.

SIMON

What about New York?

LAURIE

Isolated incident. Tokyo's solid as a rock. Blake Industries is the best its ever been. The rest of the markets will be fine. Nick and I have a plan for further expansion, once we get Arrow's empire.

SIMON

You think you will? He's putting up one hell of a fight.

LAURIE

I've always got what I wanted. It's a piece of cake.

SIMON

The rumours—

LAURIE

Who believes rumours? The thing is we just need the icing on the cake.

SIMON

Laurie, you still owe us two billion.

LAURIE

Let's make it an even four.

SIMON

I have to answer to my board, Laurie. They're already dubious in this economic climate that you can pay the two.

LAURIE

Your board? Full of wimps. Two billion, that's all. Look, I'll give you as assets, my steel industries and brewery: beer! Now that's a licence for printing money.

SIMON

I don't know, Laurie.

LAURIE

What if I don't pay a red cent of the two billion.

[*His words make* SIMON *nervous*]

SIMON

You wouldn't?

LAURIE

No skin off my nose. It's your money.

SIMON

But you owe us.

LAURIE

What's going to happen if I don't pay. You're the one who'd be in trouble. It's not your money either—it's your customers': Mr and Mrs Australia. If you don't give me more money you have no chance in hell of getting the two billion back—to make money I need money.

SIMON

It's blackmail!

[LAURIE *shrugs*]

LAURIE

Suit yourself.

[LAURIE *glances nervously at an equally apprehensive* NICK *wondering if he has overplayed his hand. There is an agonising silence. He walks away.* SIMON *pauses a moment then runs after* LAURIE.]

SIMON

Wait a minute. Two more billion, Laurie. That's a lot.

LAURIE

You'd give me two million, wouldn't you?

SIMON

Yes.

LAURIE

What's two billion. An extra couple of naughts and you know what a naught is? Nothing.

[SIMON *is rocked by the logic of this*]

I promise you, mate. The extra couple of naughts and you'll get the four billion back in no time. Right?

SIMON

The assets are the steel and beer?

LAURIE

No worries. [*Slapping him on the back*] You've just made another fortune for yourself.

SIMON

[*unsure*] I think I need a drink.

LAURIE

Yeh, go and celebrate.

[*He goes.* NICK *slithers over to* LAURIE]

NICK

You might not have remembered Laurie, but we gave the beer and steel industries as securities on loans to the National Bank.

LAURIE

[*smiling*] Yeh, I remembered.

NICK

[*ecstatically*] Brilliant! Brilliant!

LAURIE

Whose mother would allow her daughter to marry a banker? It'd be like marrying her off to a rubber chicken.

[WAITER *comes out with a bottle of Coke a Cola on a tray*]

WAITER

Mr Albert, your Coke.

[NICK *looks up and gives a howl of anger*]

NICK

You idiot!

[NICK *sinks his teeth into* WAITER's *leg*]

LAURIE

Nick! Nick!

WAITER

Get him off. Get him off!

[LAURIE *drags* NICK *away,* HENRY *retreats*]

LAURIE

What's got into you?

NICK

[*eagerly*] Did I draw blood? Did I draw blood?

LAURIE

Nick, you've got to concentrate. We've got to save Blake Enterprises.

NICK

Right. [*A tear*]I'm a bit twitchy—

LAURIE

Twitchy may not be the word.

[*A worried* HENRY *enters.*]

HENRY

Sir, the Prime Minister has left.

LAURIE

He didn't say goodbye.

HENRY

He dipped out through the kitchen.

LAURIE

[*to* NICK] Christ, his minders must have told him about Tokyo. We're in deep shit.

[*He starts to go,* NICK *grabs hold of* LAURIE's *leg*]

NICK

Laurie! I went to a fortune teller to find out about the future of the economy. I asked her about us. She looked into the crystal ball and said 'I see a wonderful, huge empire'. What happens to it? I asked. She stared at the ball a long time and said, 'I don't know. All I see is that it all goes poof!'

[NICK's *words sends a shiver up* LAURIE]

SCENE FIVE · THE LUNATICS ARE TAKING OVER THE ASYLUM

An office at the top of a skyscraper. Night. Only a small lamp illuminates the space. SIMON, *lost in worried thought, gazing at the lights of the city below, drinks a large glass of whiskey. Around him are sounds, which may be in his head, or maybe all the radios and TVs in the office are on.*

VOICES

Today, Mr Laurie Blake denied Blake Industries was in trouble. He said, in fact, he was set for expansion and the deferred dividend shares was only a temporary measure. Mr Freddie Arrow said that his investigations proved beyond a doubt that Blake Industries was so highly geared, and his debt to ratio was so enormous, that Blake Industries was finished as a going concern. Banks today expressed doubt as to Blake's financial good health. Many have indicated that Mr Blake is not going to meet this month's interest payments. People are now asking how Laurie Blake earned 231 million dollars in profit last financial year and yet paid not a cent in tax. Human rights' groups are questioning Mr Blake's financial ties with the Romanian dictatorship. The Australian stock exchange today announced that Blake Industries shares had fallen from $7.50 to 80 cents. There is speculation that the stock exchange will disbar Blake Industries.

SIMON

[*to himself*] You idiot ... there's no way out of this. Jump! Oh, my god, there is no way out. I'm lost. Done for. Everything seemed so golden ... limitless.

[LAURIE *enters, beaming*]

LAURIE

Simon!

SIMON

How did you get in here?

LAURIE

Everybody knows Laurie Blake. Great view, Simon. Christ, I wish I had an office like this. A banker's wet dream.

SIMON

Either give me four billion.

LAURIE

You know I don't cany cash on me.

SIMON

[*almost hysterical*] Leave, Laurie! Fucking leave me!

LAURIE

Come on, Simon, we're mates.

SIMON

You owe our bank four billion. Westpac two—the National two—

LAURIE

Look out there! What do you see—cranes everywhere. Most of these constructions are mine.

SIMON

They're the banks', Laurie ... our money. We won't get it back will we?

LAURIE

Of course you will. Next year you'll look out there and see millions of offices and a face in every one. I'll be raking it in. Now, to get there, all I need is another couple of noughts—

SIMON

Laurie ... with all the money you and the others owe—the country is going to go bankrupt.

LAURIE

Why in the hell do bankers always look on the gloomy side? Next year—everything will be back on its feet.

SIMON

Give me the money or get out!

LAURIE

I will. First give me another two billion and then you'll get all your money back.

SIMON

Get out!

LAURIE

Christ, you wimp! The only way I can give you back your money is for you to give me more, or else you'll get nothing back. Up house mortgages! Get the money that way.

[*Silence*]

SIMON

[*quietly*] I've been thinking of suicide, Laurie.

LAURIE

Bring on the violins ...

SIMON

I feel ashamed. I admit it. I felt the heat, the fantastic orgasm of ending up here, Laurie. But don't you understand? We've driven this country bankrupt. You can't pay us back. We took our clients' money and gave it to you—

LAURIE

With no questions asked.

SIMON

Absolutely. There will be Royal Commissions, inquiries—

LAURIE

No there won't. You bankers don't have to worry. You're the most boring people on earth—who's going to sit through your testimony?

SIMON

Laurie—I can't face myself—what have I done! I can't look my kids in the eye—

LAURIE

Get off your knees then. Simon! I need the extra naughts ...

SIMON

Get away from me, Laurie. I'm going to go to jail.

LAURIE

No one is, you fucking loser. [*Taking contract out of pocket*] Sign this.

SIMON

What is it?

LAURIE

You giving me another two billion?

SIMON

[*crying out*] No!

[SIMON *rushes at the window and bounces off it—onto the floor.* LAURIE, *relentless and savage, goes to him*]

LAURIE

All you university educated people are wimps and losers. You're not like me. I'm strong, you're weak. And if you had started out like I did as a window cleaner you would have known that this is not like the 1930s depression. You can't jump through windows—it's all double glazing now. [A *beat*] Now fucking sign this, you wuzz ...

SIMON

Can't Laurie.

LAURIE

It's easy—I'll guide your pen.

SIMON

I'd love to give you a few naughts, Laurie, but I can't—I was forced to resign an hour ago.

SCENE SIX · THE BUNKER

LAURIE's *office. Day. In the background we hear telephones ringing incessantly and hear* LAURIE's *secretary on the intercom.*

INTERCOM

Mr Blake, are you there? Mr Blake, Westpac, National and ANZ are leaving messages every fifteen minutes.

MIA

[*On the telephone*] No, I'm sorry, Mr Blake isn't here at the moment. I expect him soon. [*Different call*] Yes, Mr Thompson, I'll leave a message. [*Another call*] Yes, I'll tell him when he comes in, he's not in yet.

[LAURIE *enters, perspiring after great physical exertion*]

LAURIE

Fuck me, dead. Thirty-five stories of stairs.

INTERCOM

Mr Blake, Mr Blake, are you in yet? Four men from the Australian Securities Commission want to speak to you. They're in the outer office.

LAURIE

[*to himself*] They can sit there all day for all I care. They're on fucking taxpayer's money.

[*Goes over and picks up pile of papers*]

Shred it all.

[*In quick succession a pair of steel crutches fall from the air conditioning duct, closely followed by* NICK, *who tumbles to the floor, startling* LAURIE *who drops his papers.*]

Fuck me, Nick. You almost gave me a heart attack.

[NICK *looks even more dishevelled. He seems mightily tired. He takes out a whiskey flask and takes a gulp, grinning broadly.*]

How did you get in?

NICK

Took a lift to the thirty-sixth floor and then got down here through the air conditioning duct. [*Handing flask to* LAURIE] I heard the ASC guys were waiting for us.

[LAURIE *takes a gulp*]

INTERCOM

Mr Blake, one of your creditors says he's kidnapped your dog and unless you pay him he's going to kill it.

LAURIE

Like vultures. You heard that bloody Byzantine Girl jockey returned from Asia, saying he was tired of Asian food. He's going to be a witness saying I rigged that race. Talk about gratitude. I paid him a million over the past ten years. He shagged himself so silly, he's got even shorter. It never rains but it pours. [*A beat*] Bloody Simon let us down, he cracked.

NICK

Yeh, some can't take the pressure. Personally I eat stress for breakfast.

LAURIE

Fucking gets to me. The government can't run an economy, so what happens? A recession hits those people with their arses on the line, like us. We need a bloody Ceausescu here. At least we've got the ore deal with him.

NICK

Not any longer. On the way here I heard he'd been overthrown. He and his wife were shot.

LAURIE

He and his missus?

NICK

It'll be chaos there—we can't count on the Romanians. [*Looking out window*] Laurie, there's a guy leaning out of a window in the building opposite holding a poodle by its back legs.

LAURIE

[*lost in thought*] Uh?

[NICK's *line of vision falls*]

That's my dog! [*he runs to the window*]

NICK

Was your dog, Laurie.

LAURIE

[*shaking fist at window*] You'll never get your money now, fucker! What is bloody happening in the world?

NICK

It's chaos, Laurie. I have a new theory. It's called the chaos theory. It offers a new way of seeing order and patterns where formerly only the random, the erratic, the unpredictable could be observed. In nature the flutter of a butterfly's wings can eventually cause a cyclone. In the business world, a pencil dropped by a secretary with PMT could cause a business empire to fall.

LAURIE

You're on the talcum powder again—

NICK

Honestly, Laurie—

LAURIE

Make some calculations: Where do we stand?

[NICK *falls to the floor, takes out his pocket calculator and starts jabbing away at the buttons*]

Total up all our assets. If we had a fire sale, how much would we be in the red. How much would we owe? [*off on another tangent*] Get this, the banks are blaming me, like I held them up for it or something. They're screaming for their money.

NICK

That's the way the world ends, not with a whimper but with a banker.

LAURIE

The bankers laid down on the floor with their tongues hanging out, their legs open. [*Notices* NICK *has finished adding up*] So how are we?

NICK

If we sell all our assets ... given the fact of a fire sale in this economic climate, we'd owe ... near as I can figure out ... about 8.5.

LAURIE

[*elated*] 8.5! Piece of piss. We'll flog a couple of Picassos and that'd be it. That's fantastic. You've made my day, Nick. I'm here to tell you I was becoming a might bit worried. But 8 and a half million is pissy!

NICK

Laurie ... not millions. Billions. We'd still owe 8.5 billion.

[*The figure rattles* LAURIE. *Silence*]

LAURIE

How did the Ceausescus die again?

NICK

Firing squad. Apparently they were so eager to shoot them, they didn't wait for the command to fire.

LAURIE

It's illegal in Australia.

NICK

My guess, Laurie is what happened to the Ceausescus will be a picnic compared to what will happen to us.

LAURIE

And those fucking journalists telling the whole world we were propping up our shares with borrowings from the banks. Those hypocrites. Six months ago they were praising me for doing exactly that. And what's the front page of the *Bulletin* this week? My picture leading the list of the 100 most ugly Australians. Bloody ungrateful nation. Stabbing us tall poppies in the back.

NICK

Ring the Treasurer—tell him if we go under the whole fucking nation goes under. They want blood, Laurie. They want to draw blood.

LAURIE

I feel like Gulliver surrounded by Liverpudlians.

INTERCOM

Mr Blake, the men from the ASC know you're in there. They want to speak to you. Mr Blake? Mr Blake? [*Almost hysterically*] Laurie, I can't take it any more—I'm leaving.

LAURIE

You know what we're going to do, Nick? What my mother and me used to do. She didn't have much money and we'd do the midnight flit. Just us and one suitcase. And she'd say to me: we're doing this so we can fight another day. [*A beat*] We're going to fight another day.

NICK

It's why I like you, Laurie. They want to grind you down, but you won't let them. In fact, I more than like you. I love you.

LAURIE

Christ, Nick, don't get all sloppy like the Prime Minister. [*A beat. An idea strikes him*] A letter, Nick. A letter to the Nation. We'll have it published in all the newspapers. [*Clicking fingers,* NICK *takes out notepad and pen*] OK, then. 'A letter from Laurie Blake. My Fellow Australians. I have been out under the most searing process of public scrutiny ever endured by a public figure. Why have I been penalised and pilloried, my reputation stained ...'

NICK

[*punching air*] Way to go, Laurie!

[*Lights fade on* NICK, *as* LAURIE *addresses the audience*]

LAURIE

You all shouted my name and lined the streets when my yacht won the America's Cup, yelling out, 'Blakey! Blakey!' You all wanted to shake my hand and pat me on the back saying, 'Good on yer, Blakey'. You saw me as an ideal. An average Australian guy who through hard work made it to the top. A man whose mother was a barmaid. A man who was overweight as a child, who everyone thought would amount to nothing. But I had a dream. And I soared. I became famous. A man who was famous throughout the world as an example of Australian energy and get up and go. I feel ashamed at how eager you are to turn on me. You encouraged me—you created me. Now you're turning on me—like a nation of cowards. Well, I still believe in the Australian dream and I still believe in you. Because whatever you can accuse me of—you can never accuse me of shirking—of being a coward. Best regards to all Australians—Laurie Blake: Order of Australia.

[*Lights fade and we hear a radio report*]

RADIO

Mr Freddie Arrow, celebrating his victory, said today that entrepreneurs such as Mr Laurie Blake bankrupted Australia. Thousands of people have lost their jobs. Companies are loaded up with debt to pay for deals. Profits are sacrificed to pay interest costs on the borrowings and even so, many companies will be forced into bankruptcy or dire restructurings. Bondholders and shareholders are going to lose many millions more. Mr Freddie Arrow went on to say that this morning he purchased Mr Blake's yacht.

SCENE SEVEN · THE YELLOW BRICK ROAD

An island off the Libyan coast. NICK *is in a special brace hanging from a tree, in order to relieve the pressure on his back. He reads from a folded up newspaper in one hand and munches a cookie with the other,* BRENDA is *sunning herself. A woman dressed in a chador passes.*

BRENDA

Hey, Fatima—a cup of tea. [*Fatima takes no notice and* exits] God, if I had divorced Laurie when I had the chance I would be a millionaire. Instead, look at us. A dump on some god forsaken island, off the coast of Libya.

NICK

[NICK *takes a half chewed biscuit from pocket and gulps it down greedily*] Not bad for a dump.

BRENDA

But a dump all the same. Look at our pool. Covered in leaves and shit. I have asked for someone to come and clean it day in day out. Bloody lazy people these Arabs. [*Distant sound of the call to prayers*] If they're not sleeping they're yodelling in their temple five times a day. [*She gets up*] I remember when I had maids to go and do shopping for me. Want anything?

NICK

Yeh, don't forget my cookies.

BRENDA

Can't I get them elsewhere. His shop is so sleazy.

NICK

[*urgently*] I want my hash cookies! I want them! [*A beat, calmer*] My mash cookies and newspapers. I'm interested to see what happens to Bond.

BRENDA

He'll swing.

NICK

[*chuckling to himself*] Well, you know what a business entrepreneur is? A con man who hasn't been caught yet. But if he does swing ... it's a lesson for us.

BRENDA

What lesson?

NICK

We don't go back to Australia.

BRENDA

Australia's always coming here. Photographers jumping over the walls. Journalists banging on our door.

[LAURIE *enters*]

How did it go?

LAURIE

The owner was as useful as an aging queen with a sore throat. I go to the abattoirs to see over them—Christ, like Australia in the seventies, primitive, primitive—and I give them suggestions on how to modernise it. Make it the best in the Arabic world, but Muslims, they've got all these bloody religious rules and regulations. The other fuckin' annoying thing is how they all speak Arabic.

BRENDA

[*angrily*] You're the one who said come to Libya. You're the one who said it was a new frontier. We'll build the biggest tourist resort in North Africa. And look at us, we're just about broke.

LAURIE

That's great! That's gratitude. All the kickbacks I had to pay. How was I to know you need his and hers swimming pools.

BRENDA

You go and build the biggest bar in Africa! It's a bloody Moslem country. You can be executed for selling alcohol.

LAURIE

I had a vision—did you have one!

NICK

[*yelling*] My head! Can we stop the arguing. Day in, day out!

[*Pause*]

BRENDA

Want anything down the street?

[LAURIE *irritably shakes his head,* BRENDA *goes*]

NICK

[*shouting after her*] The cookies! The cookies!

LAURIE

You're eating a lot of biscuits.

NICK

Can't get alcohol here, so the ... sugar hit eases the pain in my back.

LAURIE

That brace is a silly idea.

NICK

Your doctor recommended it.

LAURIE

Nick—My doctor is Skase's doctor. I'm supposed to have no lungs left.

NICK

Help me down. I'm going in to see if I can get any news from Australia. Can I have my crutches?

LAURIE

No, you're a bloody menace to yourself and everyone else when you've eaten those bikkies.

[*A testy* NICK *stays in his brace and listens to his Walkman. A girl wearing a chador enters with pool cleaning equipment.*]

Yes?

CLEANER

[*pointing*] Swim. Water.

LAURIE

You've come to clean the pool?

[*She smiles happily and heads off to clean pool*]

[*Half to himself*] How does an Arab husband know if he's got a good sort or not?

[TERRY BURCHETT *enters, wearing sunglasses, and stands unnoticed watching* LAURIE. *He approaches* LAURIE, *looking much more mature and confident. He takes off his sunnies.* LAURIE *is very surprised to see him*]

Terry Burchett …

TERRY

Passing through, Laurie. I went to England first for Freddie Arrow's funeral—

LAURIE

Didn't recognise you without the frock. [*Can barely hide his pleasure*] No sea legs—slipped off the deck of the yacht he bought from me. Karma.

TERRY

Then I went on to Russia.

LAURIE

Russia?

TERRY

Part of a long term plan of mine. Russia is a loss. A mess. It's filled with all sorts of con artists and fake millionaires from the west trying to muscle in. It's like the Wild East. The greatest collection of sleazebags in the world. The whole system runs on bribery and corruption. Some of the art though, was beautiful.

LAURIE

[*picking up newspaper*] Your paper is saying some very harsh things about me, Terry.

TERRY

I bought *The Herald* for a pittance I decided to give the editor a free hand—even though I don't necessarily agree with him.

LAURIE

It constantly bashes me. Bond. Skase. Elliot. Connell. I mean, in the eighties were gods. But, you see, Australia doesn't like tall poppies—

TERRY

You left Australia with a debt of fourteen billion. That's the GNP of a small African nation.

LAURIE

[*ego involved here*] A big African nation. Nick gave me some really bad advice. I'm thinking of firing him. Anyway, why are you here?

TERRY

I came here with a proposition. The Australian Securities Commission would naturally like to talk to you back in Australia.

LAURIE

I'm a sick man.

TERRY

Miracle cures do happen. In all likelihood you wouldn't go to trial. It would be a matter of helping them track down all your assets and—

LAURIE

Make me bankrupt. I'll end up in jail.

TERRY

Jail? Not at all. At the most you'll have to pay back a cent for every hundred dollars. I can't imagine a man like you enjoying this life—

LAURIE

It's perfect one day, paradise the next.

TERRY

I care about Australia. What we have to do is try and

put it back on its feet. I don't hold grudges. I did for a while—buying the brewery from me at a weak and confusing moment of my life—but Australia comes first. Also, to be perfectly frank, the good thing was to be able to buy back the paper and brewery at bargain basement prices. You only have one Laurie Blake in your life. I discovered I valued my name and I'm going to restore it. I'm even marrying.

LAURIE

It'll be the old Lady Chatterley trick, eh?

TERRY

Whatever it takes to continue the Burchett name.

LAURIE

You're even more ruthless than me.

TERRY

You created me. You got me the day after my father's death. You got me while I was vulnerable. You've taught me to be ruthless. You're a good teacher, Laurie. I don't blame you. After all, every one had the fever. Even secretaries would open the financial pages of the paper first to see if their stock had reached new, dizzy heights. If you came back I would go easy on you in my papers.

LAURIE

Do I trust you?

TERRY

Absolutely. You'll be made bankrupt, but there will be no search for revenge.

LAURIE

You're sure about that. The ASC?

TERRY

They don't want revenge, either.

[*Pause*]

LAURIE

Why would you do this for me, Terry?

TERRY

Because I need you. Despite your crudities, your coarseness, you know about beer. Meat. Transport ... I don't. I have a private jet that's flying me back to Sydney tonight. I'd love you to be on it. Again, my newspapers would help you. They'd point out, that everyone was doing what you were doing. You were merely a reflection of the times. [*Holding out hand*] Agreed?

LAURIE

[*shaking hands*] I'll think about it.

TERRY

I can't imagine you surviving on shashlik and goats cheese.

LAURIE

Yeh, it's like being forced to watch SBS every day.

[TERRY *smiles*]

TERRY

Good to see you again, Laurie. A sight for sore eyes after Moscow.

[*He goes,* LAURIE *broods*]

LAURIE

[to *himself*] Six o'clock. Will have to move fast to get there.

NICK

[*waking up with a start*] Laurie! Laurie!

LAURIE

What is it?

NICK

I've just heard on the short wave, Bond's been sent to jail. They've got him.

LAURIE

[*half to himself*] The bastard lied.

NICK

What bastard.

LAURIE

Doesn't matter.

[*Pause*]

Well, that's it, isn't it?

BRENDA

What is?

LAURIE

It's the clink for certain if we go back to Australia.

BRENDA

For you maybe—

LAURIE

Half of those companies you theoretically own. You signed hundreds of contracts.

BRENDA

You told me to sign. I had no idea what I was doing. I can't bear it. I can't bear to be stuck here.

NICK

What'll we do, Laurie. Oh, oh, reality's intruding. I need a top up. Give me my cookies. I want my cookies!

[LAURIE *is at a loss,* NICK *snatches the cookie bag from* BRENDA's *grasp—she hardly notices—and he starts to devour a hash cookie*]

BRENDA

We're done for.

NICK

We're running out of money.

[NICK *takes out pocket calculator and starts making frantic calculations*]

BRENDA

I'm going back. I miss Australia.

LAURIE

Don't be silly, woman, they'll crucify you.

BRENDA

I'm only a housewife.

LAURIE

Of the most sought after man in Australia. The government did this to us.

NICK

[*having done calculations*] Three months at the most.

BRENDA

OK, then—we issue a statement: we don't go back to Australia until the government apologises.

NICK

[*having done calculations*] Three months at most.

LAURIE

I have an idea.

NICK

[*the top up of the hash has taken quick effect*] Yo! Laurie!

LAURIE

We're going to the Wild East.

BRENDA

Wild East?

LAURIE

There's a fortune to be made out there for people like us. Fuck Australia, what's it ever done for us. Let's start again in Russia.

NICK & BRENDA

Russia?

LAURIE

It's the beginnings of capitalism. No stupid regulations like in the West. This is a new frontier. This time capitalism will work for us. This time we'll get it right!

[NICK *gets caught up in his enthusiasm*]

NICK

Brilliant! They've only just discovered capitalism. They'll be like babes in the wood.

LAURIE

They'll be desperate for our abilities. A brand new world.

NICK

We'll teach them about the share market, the positive value of debt—

LAURIE

Leveraged buy outs—

NICK

Junk bonds—

LAURIE

Off shore companies—

BRENDA

We'll be rich again.

LAURIE

Then after ten years we'll return to Australia. Famous and rich.

BRENDA

They'll jail us, Laurie.

LAURIE

No. They'll receive us with open arms. You know why? Money has no memory. [*Fervently*] I believe we're passing through this life, ready for the next—and our next stop: Moscow. Moscow, here we come!

TRIO

MOSCOW! MOSCOW! Moscow!

THE END

HOW TO BECOME A BUSINESS ENTREPRENEUR

NICK ALBERT

CHAPTER ONE · THE PHILOSOPHY

The heating is not working properly and my window is frosted up so I cannot see outside. But there is really nothing to see, just a ratty fleamarket where Muscovites sell old clothes, broken clocks, illegal vodka, mouldy copies of Tolstoy and gnarled looking potatoes (no one touches the deformed mushrooms from the Chernobyl region). As I wait out this winter, feeling as though I am in prison, I thought I'd jot down a few notes for both Russians and any Australian thinking about embarking on a career as a business entrepreneur. As the west waits out its recession, it knows affluence is just around the comer and then winter will give way to the spring of business entrepreneurs again. And as for Russia, this guide will help those budding capitalists who want to become as famous as the Elliots, Blakes, Bonds and Holmes à Courts of Australia.

So here it is, typed laboriously with two frost bitten fingers on a monstrously heavy, 1940s, manual typewriter with a faded ribbon I bought from one of the fleamarket stalls, 'Property of KGB' engraved on its sides, the English typeface evidence of the cold war disinformation programme.

What is a business entrepreneur? A business entrepreneur is a con man who hasn't been caught yet. Like the con man, the entrepreneur appeals to the imagination of the people who give him money. Like the con man the entrepreneur takes other people's money. He is a man who has no management skills, no science skills, no patience to build up a business empire and not many ideas. In fact, he only has one idea—one great idea. That is that there are businesses which have been built up carefully and slowly over years, which have little debt—because of old fashioned ideas about not wanting to go into debt—and many assets. And such businesses are ripe for the picking.

The first thing to know is that shareholders are the key. They haven't invested in a company out of altruistic concerns, no, they want a return. So if someone can promise them a greater return, they will sell out their grandmother for it. And that's what the BE (business entrepreneur) knows. Business is the greed of humans made naked. He will appeal to the greed of others, because he himself is greedy. He knows that banks are greedy, board members are greedy, and he knows the obvious secret: business is about greed.

How does a man know he is a BE? Well, they are generally formed early. For example, look at the school playground. You can all recognise the class nerd (he will grow up to be the computer expert or Forex dealer), the swot (your banker), the teacher's pet (Securities Commission) and there's our boy. Not very good looking (e.g. Elliot's huge nose and craggy face, Bond's pre-prison beer gut, Holmes à Court's weak chin), but he's the one who spends time in metal work classes cutting out reasonable replicas of dollar coins to go in drink machine slots, he's the one who organises a shoplifting expedition but stays behind because he's going to fence the stolen property around the play-yard, he's the one who pays a friend to do an exam for him, and he's the one who leaves school before going to university because he knows that all those who go on to earn their degrees can be bought later on. Because he knows that every man has his price.

He will leave school to sell TVs with only one channel, start real estate firms selling dismal blocks of land renaming Marsh Flats as Paradise and Barren Ridge as Babylon Hills. And eventually he comes to the realisation that to start one's business and work at building it up over twenty or thirty years takes too long. He is an impatient man. It is easier to take over someone else's business and in the classic example the BE will take over a business that has been built up over one or two generations. The BE will tell the world that the business is staid and old fashioned and that he will bring new management skills to it and will modernise.

Before we get to the art of the takeover it is important to ask yourself if you have the psychological make-up of a corporate predator. This man realises that to make it he has to have an insatiable appetite for money and for takeovers. Once started he cannot stop. He will know that there are only two important emotions in business: greed and fear, and he will play on both, knowing full well that people react to fear, they wallow in love. He knows that a weak man urges compromise, a strong man never does. He knows that the heaven of achievement is paved with bad intentions. He knows that the name of the game is not to win friends, but to win. He must have a consuming eagerness for the fray. Alan Bond used to actually dribble with excitement and enthusiasm. It was his way of showing keenness but Red, his wife, told him to stop it, because she thought it was a disgusting habit. He also knows that patience is another word for laziness and above all, the BE knows one basic truth: if you can't be a builder, become a taker.

BE and capitalism go together because socialism is for people who can't make it as capitalists. If there is one thing that binds all people, whatever their religion or politics, it is money. The language of money needs no translation and the wonderful thing is that money has no morality and no memory. People say, 'What about the people who have no money?' The BE knows that God hates the poor, why else would he let them live in misery? But is not the hunger for money another word for greed? Let's answer that with a quote from Conrad Black, BE, 'Greed has been severely underestimated and denigrated, unfairly so, in my opinion. And how do you make money? By becoming successful. Success is God's way of telling you that you are a success. What is the purpose of having money—to buy and to spend. Anyone who lives within their means is suffering from a lack of imagination. Money is the art of making the most out of life.'

In taking over a business remember a corporate raider is a predator. But he must hide this under a charming facade. He must hold out the lure of huge earnings for shareholders, the firm commitment that no one will lose their job and he must make big plans, because no one responds to small plans. Talk about a vision for the future of the company. The BE will enter on his quest with a gut feeling. Market research is for cowards. He also knows that when he becomes well known for his takeovers and others hear about his raid on a company, the situation will resemble the feeding frenzy of a school of piranhas let loose at a school swimming carnival. So even when he's at the top he still has to be the greatest predator of them all.

But what if you have no money when you start out. No problem! Go to a bank. Learn a lesson from Australia in the eighties. The first principle of borrowing is that it becomes easier the more money you want to borrow. If you want a billion, it is easier to get than a thousand as every ordinary person knows when asking for a loan. When the sums are large enough, avarice takes over. The bankers are blinded, bedazzled by the lure of profits. Bankers, generally sad sacks at the best of times, want their posh cars and apartments too. At the height of the boom banks were desperate to loan. The more they loaned, the larger they got. The bigger they grew, the greater their status in the banking community—which is what mattered most to them. What if you go into debt? This is where banks are at their best. A thousand dollar debt is your problem, a billion dollar debt is theirs. The more debt a BE has, the more banks will give him in the hope that he can buy into more companies, sell off the assets and pay back the original loan. And remember, when your empire is in the black, it's your money, when you are desperately in the red, it's the bank's money.

In the takeover the first thing is to strip the company of its assets, after all, because you have no money, it is the only way to pay back the loan—or, in reality, pay the interest on the loan. Not only will you have to sell off assets but you will have to fire some staff. Remember, a single person fired is a tragedy, a thousand is a statistic. To justify this, call it 'Restructuring'. It's important to go into a takeover with a thoroughly realistic attitude. There are three ways of looking at the takeover. First is to destroy the target company by completely stripping it of assets, and view it as the Americans did. When in Vietnam they were fond of saying, 'We had to destroy the village in order to save it'. The second way is to take personal command of the company yourself, of course, you have little time to do that. Or there is the third option and that is to appoint someone to do your wishes (see notes on Leadership and Aides below).

When taking over the target company the BE should calculate the sum of all injuries he will have to do and do them all at once, so as not to have to do new ones every day. If the BE does his damage quickly then there will be less time to dwell on the injuries. And, most importantly, if you injure someone, better not do it by halves, or else sometime, somewhere down the financial track the BE will have to deal with that person again.

How to treat the staff? Again, like most things to do with takeovers, it is about psychology. A few hints though from the example of Laurie Blake: Keep executives in line by having them sign undated letters of resignation to be filled in at the appropriate date. Have cameras focused on the photocopy machines to watch for staff copying information for another firm. In the Forex and trader sections, both of which have a high burn-out factor, hire men who are unhappy, short, insecure, preferably with a failed marriage behind them. They are losers always looking to prove themselves the best. They want to be the richest and the most well known on the financial block. All they end up with is a pair of platform shoes, on the dole before they're forty and a temporary wife with big tits who takes all their money for alimony. You see, the socially awkward Forex dealer is a nerd thinking he is getting revenge on the world when all he is is a screen jockey with a work lifespan of five years.

But surely there is staff loyalty? Loyalty is people wanting their end of year bonus. And a friend is just a potential enemy. What of trust? LBJ once said he never trusted a man 'unless I've got his pecker in my pocket'. My advice is don't even trust him then, because in all likelihood he's going to piss in it. A man will say anything before the takeover and during it, just as he will say 'I love you' to a woman before and during sex, anything just to get into her pants. You will need an Aide, an off-sider, a sidekick, you can trust to take care of the details etc. Livy said there were three sorts of brains: one that understands on its own, another one that understands what people tell it and the third sort of brain is the one that understands neither itself or other people (invariably the latter go on to get MBA degrees). Try and choose the first or second type of brains. The Aide is important in a takeover because you can use him to make sure any cruel behaviour is not coming from you, but your Aide. Be careful of two things, however, in your choice of Aide. The man that makes another one powerful ruins himself. And when your Aide starts using 'I' instead of 'We', keep a close watch on him or fire him because he is starting to serve his own interests and is seeing himself as separate from you.

Closely allied to Aides are your accountants. If you wish to pay as little tax as possible, the answer is easy. Go into the enemy's camp. Buy the best men in the tax department and make them your advisers. They know more about the avoidance of tax than anyone.

There is no need for me to tell you about appearances. Once you have made it as a BE then appearance is all important. If you want to be known as a generous man then you must seize every opportunity to display it. However, adjust this to the temper of the times. For example, during a recession cultivate fake frugality.

If you're selling a mud hill spray it green and call it Hollywood Hills. It's surprising how many people finds depths in the shallowness of appearances. Never go second class, even when broke, because someone is bound to see you and, of course, if you can contemplate going second class, then you are thinking second class. Adjust to the temper of the nation or state. In football mad Melbourne Elliot supported a football team, Bond funded the America's Cup victory (many people remember where they were when JFK was shot, most Australians remember where they were when they heard of Australia 2's victory). Cultivate patriotism and tell the nation your first thoughts are for the good of the country.

Your image is vital to you, just as financial journalists are vital to the maintaining of this image. Financial journalists are the junk bonds of journalism. They adore success and they want to be a part of it, either by becoming a corporate raider themselves like Skase, or just enjoying being in the presence of a BE. Most of them have as much knowledge of how the economy works as economists (see below). In Australia they helped create the BE as legend. We are grateful to them. Feed them sparingly, give them 'scoops'. If by chance they become nosy ignore them and give exclusive interviews to magazine feature writers who don't even pretend to know about economics.

Politicians are easy to cultivate. They love success. They can be sickeningly full of praise for you like Prime Minister Hawke was towards Bond, Packer and the rest, but those are the hazards of dealing with such creatures. Remember, the Prime Minister or President is not the most important person in government—the Treasurer is. You must cultivate him with all the care in the world. He is the one who can save you with special tax breaks or allow off-shore trading. Pretend to believe every word he says; there is no more surprised and grateful politician than one who is believed. Money has no ideology. As one BE once said: 'When I deal with people in Canberra, I don't stop to ask myself are they Labor or Liberal? As far as I'm concerned they are businessmen like myself'.

Economists are clairvoyants gazing into shattered crystal balls. They are like doctors who tell a woman after she has accidentally gotten pregnant that her partner should have worn a condom. An economist is someone who gets his forecast right five years after the event. The golden rule is that an economist knows nothing until after the event. All economics is psychology and rumours. A share market drop is caused by rumour and gossip not by economic knowledge.

What about that other prize of power? Women. Women will want to be with even the ugliest BE. Why? Because as the present Mrs Conrad Black once said: 'Power is an aphrodisiac because it protects and offers a shield from the world. It envelops a woman and plays to her most basic instinct of vulnerability. Power is sexy, not simply in its own right, but because it inspires self confidence in its owner and a shiver of subservience on the part of those who approach it.' In other words, money is the root of all women. If there is a common language between men and women then it is money. Even marriage does not stop other women from wanting to be with you. As Laurie Blake once said, 'Marriage is an institution and I feel like I've been certified'. And as many other BEs know, marriage does not stop you from playing around in the best hotels in the world. As Laurie Blake has said: 'Experience is the best lecher'.

But what of ideals and ethics? The first thing is the most obvious: business ethics is a contradiction in terms. What is also obvious is that if you tried to be good all the time you are bound to come to grief because the world is full of men who are not good, hence a BE must learn how not to be good. It's only illegal in business if you don't get away with it. What is wonderful about Australia is the concept of mateship. In America plea bargaining mixed with the notion that there is no such thing as mateship means that the yankees frequently sell each other out. In Australia the lowest of the low is an informer which means the Securities Commission can never get a BE to rat on another BE. I suppose this could be called ethics. As you quickly learn in the cut-throat world of takeovers, prejudice saves thinking time. But a BE has to be careful of his image. Oppose capital punishment (but keep it to yourself that the reason you do is that hanging is too good for criminals), support Greenpeace (because you can earn kudos and wipe the donation off in tax). Take an Australian example of someone who doesn't have what it takes to become a BE: Western Mining Chief Hugh Morgan speaks out constantly against Aboriginal rights. A BE would support them, but secretly mine sacred sites. Morgan creates focus on what his company is doing in Aboriginal areas. No wonder he doesn't have what it takes to become a BE. In the world of takeovers beware of the man with pure motives. The purer the motives, the more dangerous a person is. And what about a person who urges caution and talks of ethics? Then that man is an appeaser and an appeaser is someone who thinks a serial killer is someone just going through a phase in their lives.

Now we come to the crucial question of leadership. There are the obvious qualities: energy, blame others for failures, fail to give credit, promises are made to be broken, leaders who live by the rules die by the rules, only take no for an answer when it is a yes, make people obliged to you, delegate unpleasant jobs to others and give yourself the pleasant duties etc. But there are other aspects to Leadership. Remember without action a leader cannot act and principles slow down action. Panic is the first resort of the born loser. You can never tell a BE he is wrong in front of his inferiors, unless you want to destroy him. Have advisers but those men only give advice when asked. Fire those who give uncalled for advice—it doesn't matter if the advice is right or not, the fact is that you didn't ask for it. A BE takes counsel and no one gives advice until asked for it.

A man's name, say old salesmen, is to him the sweetest in the world. Use it all the time and if you want to insult him, pretend to forget it, especially in front of others (a good technique with uppity bankers, the other alternative is to abuse them over the telephone when they're pleading for their money—this is called Phone Terrorism). Now, back to an earlier point: is it better to be loved or feared? To be feared is much safer because it involves the threat of punishment and people dread punishment. Is this cruel? No, it is merely another technique. People condemn the cruelty of some of the actions of Alexander the Great, yet they admire his accomplishments. The thing is, he could never have succeeded without the former. It is important to note that deceit is a legitimate weapon of the BE. Men are so simple and so dominated by immediate needs that a deceitful BE will always find plenty of people who are ready to be deceived. Returning to the question of trust and leadership: Rule with men you don't trust. Unlike trustworthy men they want to work hard to earn your trust.

The other major aspect of BE leadership, especially in the modern world, is Chaos. Leadership by Chaos. Entropy is the end of all human activities. Avoid it by creating the energy of chaos. Therefore, follow impulse rather than clearly defined corporate goals. Like a genius film director give contradictory orders. You are not in the business of creation, you are in the business of creative destruction. In nature there is chaos. Chaos theory offers a new way of seeing order and patterns where formerly only the random, the erratic, the unpredictable could be observed. In nature the butterfly's wings can eventually cause a cyclone. In the business world, a pencil dropped by a secretary with PMT can cause an empire to fall. In other words, everything is based on chaos—use it as your strength. Calendars are an invention of the human imagination, invent your own. If in financial trouble, invent a new financial year, for example, one that goes from December to March. They changed the calendar during the middle ages, so can you. Just when people are getting used to your good humour, shout at them, just when they think they know what suits you like get others completely different. Make sure people never take you for granted. The basic music of the 20th century is atonal. It seems chaotic but there is a sort of structure underneath it: in business chaos also has an underlining structure: we call it Greed.

Next chapters include: 'How to Stage a Takeover', 'How to

Avoid Paying Taxes', 'The Romance of Offshore Companies', 'Who's the Greater Nerd: Banker or Head of the Australian Securities Commission', 'Choosing a Football Team', 'Buying Old Masters', 'Bankruptcy: Curse or Salvation?', 'Managers are a Dime a Dozen', 'The Board or See How the Blind Mice Run', 'Financial Journalists: Sycophants or Dupes?' 'Other People's Money' and 'Who Has the Biggest Cock on the Block: The Inner Psychology of Business Entrepreneurs'.

COPYRIGHT

First published in 1993 by Currency Press

This edition published in 2021 by Ligature Pty Limited
34 Campbell St · Balmain NSW 2041 · Australia
www.ligatu.re · mail@ligatu.re

e-book ISBN: 9781922749390

ligature *un*tapped

This print edition published in collaboration with Brio Books, an imprint of Booktopia Group Ltd

Level 6, 1A Homebush Bay Drive · Rhodes NSW 2138 · Australia

Print ISBN: 9781761281648

briobooks.com.au

brio BOOKS

MIX
Paper from responsible sources
FSC® C008194
FSC www.fsc.org

The paper in this book is FSC® certified. FSC® promotes environmentally responsible, socially beneficial and economically viable management of the world's forests.